EMPOWERMENT

"At last! An approach to personal growth that vguides us beyond mere understanding of how our lives are not working. This book is innovative and courageous, on the cutting edge of self development. It is for people who are ready to manifest their visions in the everyday world."

—Joseph Jastrab, therapist, workshop leader, and author of *Sacred Manhood, Sacred Earth*

"This book is powerful, practical, and clear. It will heal and empower those of us who are solving our yesterdays and creating our todays and tomorrows."

—Gerald G. Jampolsky, M.D., author, *Love Is Letting Go of Fear*

"Personal Empowerment may well be the key to our collective survival. The authors, creators of the massive global initiative, the First Earth Run, have addressed the issue of personal empowerment not just theoretically but practically."

—Marilyn Ferguson, author, *The Aquarian Conspiracy*

"I have experienced real change in my life since reading and doing the exercises in your Empowerment book. I don't know if other people notice it as well, but I feel stronger, and more capable. I can recognize my fears now as they arise in me, and then question their validity. For the first time in my working life, I raised my voice at an insubordinate employee; it felt great. I have just completed writing a long letter to my parents discussing subjects I never dared discuss. I feel more empowered than I ever have."

—Richard Brown, Columbus, Ohio

"It's time to inform you, which I do with great pleasure, about what has happened since I finished my research on the relationship between quality development and empowerment. I used your book *Empowerment* to develop a model for organizations in which the process of 'permanent improvement' and 'keeping on the growing edge' go hand in hand. In my training programs for organizations, I am finding excellent results using your *Empowerment* book and tools."

—Connie Schijf, Leiden, The Netherlands

EMPOWERMENT

The Art of Creating Your Life as You Want It

SECOND EDITION

David Gershon & Gail Straub

STERLING

New York / London
www.sterlingpublishing.com

STERLING and the distinctive Sterling logo are registered trademarks of Sterling Publishing Co., Inc.

Library of Congress Cataloging-in-Publication Data

Gershon, David.
 Empowerment : the art of creating your life as you want it / David Gershon and Gail Straub. -- 2nd ed.
  p. cm.
 ISBN 978-1-4027-6455-4
 1. Self-realization. 2. Visualization. I. Straub, Gail. II. Title.
 BF637.S4G47 2011
 158--dc22

2010034606

10 9 8 7 6 5 4 3 2 1

Published by Sterling Publishing Co., Inc.
387 Park Avenue South, New York, NY 10016
This edition is based on material found in *Empowerment* ©1989 by David Gershon and Gail Straub
© 2011 by David Gershon and Gail Straub
Distributed in Canada by Sterling Publishing
c/o Canadian Manda Group, 165 Dufferin Street
Toronto, Ontario, Canada M6K 3H6
Distributed in the United Kingdom by GMC Distribution Services
Castle Place, 166 High Street, Lewes, East Sussex, England BN7 1XU
Distributed in Australia by Capricorn Link (Australia) Pty. Ltd.
P.O. Box 704, Windsor, NSW 2756, Australia

Sterling ISBN 978-1-4027-6455-4

3 9547 00360 1528

For information about custom editions, special sales, premium and corporate purchases, please contact Sterling Special Sales Department at 800-805-5489 or specialsales@sterlingpublishing.com.

Contents

Preface to the Second Edition vii

Prologue. ix

Part One: Getting Ready

Chapter 1: Introduction to Empowerment 2

Chapter 2: Crafting Reality with Thought 19

Chapter 3: Personal Power. 40

Chapter 4: Core Beliefs 57

Part Two: The Journey

Chapter 5: Emotions. 78

Chapter 6: Relationships. 92

Chapter 7: Sexuality 108

Chapter 8: The Body. 125

Chapter 9: Money. 147

Chapter 10: Work 164

Chapter 11: Spirituality. 186

Part Three: Returning Home

Chapter 12: Always Growing! Making Your Passion Happen . . . 212

Epilogue. 223

Acknowledgments 231

Afterword. 233

Index 235

About the Authors. 240

Preface to the Second Edition

Three decades ago, the idea of empowerment was fresh and daring. As young as the word itself, we both felt that empowerment would be at the heart of our life's work. In our earliest days together, sitting with yellow legal pads at our kitchen table overlooking the Ashokan reservoir and the Catskill mountains, we planned our wedding ceremony and then seamlessly turned to designing our fledgling Empowerment Workshop. So intertwined was our love with our passion for this work, that ten days after we were married, we launched our first workshop. As we celebrate our thirtieth wedding anniversary, our bond of love is stronger than ever and our passion for empowerment more compelling than ever.

All those years ago, neither we, nor the world, knew what empowerment really meant. We knew it was about helping people to grow and realize their full potential. We also knew that it was about more than just healing and fixing problems. But what exactly was its purpose? Why was this idea entering the lexicon of change strategies with such force? Over these three decades, an extraordinarily diverse, visionary, and committed community of people was attracted to our training programs to help us discover the answers to these questions.

They came to learn for themselves, their families, their communities, their organizations, and their causes. They came from all over North America, Europe, and Latin America, but also from Afghanistan, Darfur, Rwanda, South Africa, China, Russia, and India. They included social entrepreneurs, community organizers, and environmentalists; Fortune 500 corporate leaders, organizational change consultants, and business school professors; life coaches, health-care professionals, therapists, educators, and clergy; nonprofit managers, government executives, and politicians; young and old, male and female, and embodying every race and ethnicity. In short, they represented the full diversity of our planet.

They became a global empowerment laboratory, helping us both refine our empowerment methodology and showing us the breadth for its application in society. The heart of our learning was distilled into one line: *Personal empowerment is the foundation of societal transformation.* If we wish to change our community, our organization, or the world, we must begin by changing ourselves. And the key to changing ourselves is being willing to dream a different possibility for our lives, and learning how to bring that dream to fruition. That is the essence of this book and the empowerment journey upon which you are embarking.

As you take this journey and dare to dream new possibilities for your life, know that you are also participating in a global empowerment movement—a movement that aspires to nothing less than changing the world one person and one dream at a time. And as you receive the torch passed from the many who have helped light the way before you, we hope you will do the same for others. We pass you the torch and wish you well.

David Gershon
Gail Straub

Prologue

One January evening in 1981, we went to Arnold's Turtle, one of our favorite Manhattan restaurants to eat, enjoy each other's company, and have one of our marathon talks about our future life together. We had met, fallen in love, and decided to get married in the autumn of 1980.

As we discussed our work, we realized that our individual workshops shared the common goal of helping people become more empowered. While empowerment was not a word bandied about much at the time, we were both struck by the fact that it was the principal idea that underlay both our teaching philosophies. That's when it dawned on us: One of the reasons we had come together was to combine what we each had learned about empowerment to create a new and coherent body of knowledge that we could present in the form of an intensive personal growth workshop—the Empowerment Workshop—the program upon which this book is based.

For me, Gail, my parents set the tone for my path of growth and learning. I received a profound love and curiosity about spirituality and the inner life from my mother. Her spiritual life was rich and she had a remarkable ability to impart that love of spirit without guilt. As a child, I loved talking to her about guardian angels, God, and why the sky was so blue. I learned about love from the example of her life; she was one of the most loving people I have ever known.

I developed a keen sense of social responsibility and a deep desire to create a better world from my father, who taught me very early on to ask, "Why is the world out of balance and what can I do about it?" He encouraged me to find my own answers and to understand that my actions counted. He was a man of integrity who taught me to base my life choices on that virtue.

The blending of these two precious gifts—the path of spirit walked by my mother and the path of action walked by my father—

has continued to be the major theme of my life. Between the ages of five and eighteen, I was blessed with an outstanding education that was well balanced in its attention to the mental, emotional, physical, and spiritual aspects of learning. Though I didn't realize it until many years later, this education imbued me with the understanding that the learning process is a holistic, multidimensional experience.

Living among different cultures was one of the major rites of passage in my life. By the time I turned twenty-four, I had lived and worked in South America, Europe, and Africa. Each was a significant classroom; from each one I developed my enduring love and deep respect for Earth's diversity. My experience of other cultures was also my first exposure to the concept that different belief systems create different realities, an idea that later formed the conceptual basis of the Empowerment Workshop.

I spent time with the Peace Corps in West Africa, an experience that awakened me to the reality of how most of the people on our planet live. It's an understatement to say that this way of living was a shock to my middle-class American sensibilities; yet my African friends taught me about much more than hardship. They taught me about joy, softness, sensuality, and the magic of simply being alive. I might never have found these spiritual gifts had I not stepped out of our goal-oriented Western culture.

I left Africa by crossing the Sahara Desert by camel and truck. It was a remarkable physical crossing, but it was also a symbolic crossing—the passage to a new chapter in my life. I was scared and confused and never knew what would come next on that trip. But I met someone who introduced me to two practices that would become central to my life: meditation and therapy.

I began meditation training soon after returning to the United States. Since then I have had different teachers and have gone through many ups and downs in my spiritual practice, but meditation still remains precious to me. I find that my daily connection with the silence, or what I call "the mystery," continues to nurture, heal, and balance me in ways that have become essential parts of my life.

Through therapy, I discovered that I had to uncover and heal the places where I hurt or was afraid in order to become whole. I learned that it takes courage and patience to change unconscious parts of myself. I discovered how hard I had been on myself, how to love myself exactly the way I am, and the joy of self-acceptance. And, I might add, I'm still learning all of the above!

I was introduced to the human potential movement, and what started out as a mild interest soon developed into a lifelong passion. I began to read books, take workshops, learn about many therapies, and search for mentors. This eclectic approach taught me several things, many of which found their way into the Empowerment Workshop. I became convinced that all the mental, emotional, physical, and spiritual aspects of the human condition must be considered and integrated during the process of personal growth and that there is no one way to grow: We each need to find our own path to truth. The teachers who taught me the most didn't tell me how or what to believe, but encouraged me to look deeply inside myself and, above all, to simply stay alert and alive.

As my inner development deepened, I began to yearn for a way to express some of what I had been learning through meaningful action. I had been intensely involved in the antiwar movement during my university days and, a decade later, the women's movement swept across America with its empowering message. I felt called to respond to that message and began working with various groups of women.

I found that people grow most easily in loving, joyful, and playful environments. I also discovered that many of the women I came across were in touch with their pain, but were also stuck in their pain and unable to move beyond it. I helped them create and implement new visions for their lives that had the power to heal by moving them beyond their pain into a more joyful and healthier existence.

One particular group has played an instrumental role in my growth. This circle of women, called Helix, is a place where I can safely bring all of me, a place where I am healed and nourished. Among the many things these cherished friends have taught me is that in order to give to others and the world at large, I must first love and care for myself.

In 1980, my personal growth took a quantum leap. I was in New York City leading a training session on play when an extremely attractive man named David caught my eye. One of my earliest memories of this man, who would turn out to be my husband and the love of my life, was fighting a passionate duel with Styrofoam swords that we used as part of our training. The play and dynamic tension of our co-creation started very early!

The journey of creating both marriage and life work together is not for the faint of heart. My partnership with David has been the most challenging and rewarding learning experience of my life. We continue to teach each other the lessons of love, forgiveness, balance of power, honoring our differences, and how precious we are to each other. Our empowerment work has been deeply enriched precisely because we are different.

For me, David, I was fortunate in having had a loving and secure childhood, nurtured by parents who provided me with lots of room to grow in my own way. They taught me to be open to new ideas and to seek my own path through life. I saw myself as an explorer of all that life had to offer. This exploration got truly exciting in 1968 during my senior year of college. I was majoring in international economics when it occurred to me that there had to be more to life than material well-being. It was also a year when the Beatles were in their prime and had begun to explore the world of meditation and mysticism. A big fan of their music, I decided to investigate some of the other things they were doing, which started me on a new path to greater self-awareness. As I began experimenting with meditation, yoga, and Eastern thought, I discovered new and compelling ideas and philosophies of life.

After spending nearly a year practicing meditation and reading books on spirituality, I found myself at a crossroads. The Eastern point of view seemed to suggest that the world was an illusion and our purpose was to transcend mundane life and move on to a higher state of consciousness, while the Western point of view seemed to stress that we must learn to function effectively in this world in order to improve our material existence. These two opposing perspectives forced me to choose and, for the first time in my life, I had to make a decision and commit to a belief. Even at twenty-one, I sensed that this decision would influence how I would choose to spend the rest of my life. I chose to balance the two points of view by integrating a life of spiritual development with one grounded in the material—or practical—world.

The next important crossroads on my path occurred with the discovery of an obscure book on metaphysics. This book taught that our thoughts create our experiences in life and provided readers with a number of useful exercises to help practice its principles. I followed them—and they worked. I knew I had discovered something important.

I began reading every book I could find on the art and science of affirmation, visualization, and manifestation. Reading about and experimenting with these principles and techniques made me realize that I had discovered an important part of my life's work—teaching people how to articulate and manifest a vision. Soon I was incorporating these ideas into my management training and workshops. I also continued to test them in my own life, refining my knowledge through personal experience.

As I learned these principles and techniques, I continued to search for a spiritual component for my life. I wanted to learn more about meditation in order to connect with a deeper part of myself. I found a spiritual teacher who helped me to develop spiritually and I studied with him for a number of years. Eventually, I moved on, having learned what I could from him and after I realized that his teaching style emphasized dependency. I knew I had to break away if I were to spiritually develop in my own way.

Being on my own spiritually was confusing at first, because I hadn't fully developed a sense of self. So this became the starting point on my journey of self-discovery and the moment when I began to learn how to trust in my own ability to find what was right for me. That became the goal of the next leg of my journey.

I took a number of human potential training programs and, through them, got in touch with the psychological and emotional aspects of my nature, neither of which had been addressed in my prior metaphysical and spiritual training. I had been taught that I did not need to address these aspects of my life because meditation enables us to "transcend" emotional and psychological issues. So I wound up either repressing or transcending quite a lot of my life. I also discovered that my ability to use metaphysical and spiritual knowledge effectively was largely dependent on my psychological and emotional development. This realization formed the next major piece in my evolving understanding of personal growth and human potential.

As I continued on my path of self-development, I began to feel a need to bring this work into the larger world. I joined an international organization associated with the United Nations whose mission was bringing people together to tackle the many issues facing humanity. Working with this organization was the beginning of a major commitment I made in an effort to help bring about positive change in the world. I had now found the final piece of the puzzle—a social context for my work helping people realize their potential. Over the years I have continued to use the human potential knowledge I have gained both to improve the world and as part of my training programs for business, communities, and the public at large.

So, as Gail and I talked on that special evening at Arnold's Turtle, my vision of empowering others was well-established. I wanted to help people experience their full human potential—physically, emotionally, mentally, and spiritually—both personally and in the greater context of the global community. Our great dance of partnership—commingling our learning experiences and our male and female perspectives—was about to begin.

In October 1981, just ten months after that conversation, Gail and I conducted our first Empowerment Workshop in Boston. Since then, the workshop has been our greatest teacher. It has taught us how each of us is unique while sharing the common bond of the human condition. This has afforded us the two gifts of perspective and empathy about our shared humanity.

We dedicate this book to the thousands of Empowerment Workshop graduates who have enriched our lives and our teaching through the courage and nobility of spirit they demonstrated in reaching out to achieve their full potential as human beings. And we offer this book to you, our reader, with the belief that it will also help you develop your fullest potential as a human being.

PART ONE

Getting Ready

Introduction to Empowerment

Buckle up! You are about to embark on a life adventure. It will call forth from you inner resources you may never have known you had. It will help free you of self-imposed limitations. It will provide you with the means to shape your own destiny. You will learn the art of creating your life as you want it.

Most of us settle for far less in our lives than we are capable of achieving. We fall victim to impoverished dreams, dreams that don't begin to do justice to our potential. We need to learn how to dream; how to boldly and courageously reach for our highest visions. This book will help you dare to dream and, equally important, give you the necessary skills and tools to realize these dreams. You will learn how to harness the passion of your heart and the power of your mind and express your full potential. The process of accomplishing this we call empowerment.

On this journey of empowerment, you will discover what it is you really want for your life. Discovering what you want is often a revelation in itself. Knowing your deepest heart can mean avoiding years spent pursuing other people's dreams.

Once you have a life vision worthy of your fullest effort, you will learn techniques to transform limiting beliefs and bring your life vision into full manifestation. If you engage wholeheartedly, you will come away from this journey feeling alive in a way you may never have thought possible.

Watering the Seeds, Not the Weeds

Why is it that so few people are willing to dream boldly, to reach for their highest visions?

Part of the reason is that our culture is primarily pathologically based. It focuses on what is *wrong* with a person. Many therapies consider success to be helping people get "better," with *better* being defined as the absence of neurosis. There is rarely a direct focus on full potential or optimum well-being.

This is not a condemnation of these therapies; rather, it is a sober look at our dominant cultural belief. This belief assumes a view of life in which each of us learns merely how to cope and fit in rather than to excel and move out. Much of the personal growth work that has evolved over the past few decades reflects this dominant pathological attitude of our culture. This approach is rather like a gardener who spends so much time finding and pulling weeds that she ignores the planting, care, and cultivation of fruitful plants.

If you have gone through some of these therapies or growth experiences, you will probably know why your life *doesn't* work—in great detail. You will have developed a theory as to what caused you to be the way you are now and learned some tools for coping. This work is valuable and important, in that it does help you cope more effectively with problems in your life.

However, it needs to go further. Knowing that the reason you feel insecure is that your father withheld love from you when you were a child and learning how to accept this are just the first steps. Developing the self-love and inner resources to feel secure and confident throughout your life is another matter entirely, and you must learn the ways of this new world if you are to express your full potential.

We call this other world creating a *vision* for your life. To create an inspired life vision, we must develop an acute awareness of the possibilities that lie within us. Until we do this, our potential remains dormant.

The empowerment growth process is effective because it helps you to:

- Overcome the places in your life where you are having problems.

- Discover and manifest your fullest possibility as a human being.

Specifically, it teaches you how to transform the limiting beliefs and behavior patterns that are causing you difficulties. And then it helps you release and direct your creative energies toward achieving what you really want—from a healthier body to better relationships; from material success to a richer spiritual life.

We refer to this shift as moving from *pathology* to *vision*. It is shifting our basic attitude toward life from problem solving to vision crafting. For many of us, this is a subtle and dramatic shift. It requires us to let go of the deep, problem-oriented programming of our culture and accept the belief that we can and will create the life we want.

One person who went through this shift described it in the following way: "With the empowerment process I challenged myself to move away from the safe and familiar world of my problems. I developed the specific skills for exploring the risky, exciting, and positive frontier of creating what I want in my life."

Making this powerful a change in perspective is more than a simple overnight process. It takes time and requires us to be patient and compassionate with ourselves as we learn how to think and act in this dynamic new way.

Reasons for Your Journey

There are many reasons people choose to take this journey. The following list of reasons comes from people who have taken our Empowerment Workshop. See if any of these motivations ring true for you.

- I'm in a time of transition and I need to focus on what's next.
- I need to learn how to deal with money.
- I need to take better care of myself.
- I want to attract a lasting relationship.
- I want to learn how to visualize; I've been hearing about it for years.

- I want to learn about me.
- I'm interested in the power of attitude and the changes it brings.
- I've got a lot of inner shoveling to do, and I need to muster the courage to do it.
- I want to apply my personal growth interests in my workplace.
- I'm stuck in many areas of my life.
- I want to stop pulling the rug out from under myself whenever I get close to success.
- I want to learn how to focus on my goals and clarify what I want.
- I want to move away from concentrating on my problems.
- I have been asleep and it is time to wake up.
- I want to discover my spirituality.
- I have been too preoccupied with my work and want to find a way to be more balanced so I can discover the rest of my life.

Once a person has gone through the empowerment process, creative breakthroughs and dynamic self-growth begin to occur. The following stories come from people who took our Empowerment Workshop. They are examples of the kinds of challenges people confronted and the positive changes they brought about in their lives.

Janice had just ended yet another relationship. She felt devastated, sad, and alone. She had seen this pattern to her breakups before, and this time she felt as though she didn't have the energy to pick herself up and try again.

Through the empowerment process, Janice began to examine her deep beliefs about loving herself and others. She slowly recognized how harshly she judged herself and how many beliefs she held about not being a worthy or good enough person. She realized how her own beliefs—conscious and unconscious—sabotaged her ability both to love and to be loved. She learned more about her true self, not the self she thought she was supposed to be. She began the process of forgiving herself and others and building new life-affirming beliefs about herself.

When the workshop ended, Janice was clearer about both what she wanted from a relationship and what she had to offer. She was much more realistic about the hard work, commitment, and ongoing self-love required to make a relationship successful. Janice continued to use the empowerment process daily and attracted into her life a healthy, loving, and enduring relationship.

Lou came to the Empowerment Workshop with a prestigious job he had worked hard to achieve. He also had a good marriage and family life, yet he felt empty; something wasn't right. He felt as though his life was on automatic pilot and all the passion was gone. This confused him because it seemed as if he had everything society said he needed to be happy. He kept saying to himself, "I don't have the right to be unhappy." Yet he knew in his heart there was something essential missing in his life.

With the same dedication he used to create success in his professional life, Lou dove into the empowerment process. With the help of the exercises, he reexamined his basic attitudes and premises about life. He looked closely at the life he had created for himself. He found that while he had devoted tremendous energy to taking care of his external life of family, home, and job, he had ignored his internal life—feelings, reverence, wonder, spirit, and connection with the mystery of life. Lou was out of balance in a way that is typical of people in our culture. All the emphasis is put on the active state of "doing" while the receptive state of "being" is ignored.

With the assistance of the empowerment tools, he began to nourish his interior life. He created time with his family each week in which they could share their feelings and deeper thoughts with one another. He slowed down and spent more time with nature. Lou began learning the fine art of being: a soft, receptive state of mind in which he felt content in the moment without having to do or reach for more. After several months of genuine commitment to this new orientation, a profound shift took place. Lou felt more joy than he had ever remembered. He had a new verve in his work, more love to offer his family, and peace of mind. He had created balance between his outer and inner life.

Michael was an engineer with twenty years of experience in his field. Like Lou, Michael had a feeling of inertia, low energy, and a lack of joy in his life. Though their problems were similar, the empowerment process led Lou and Michael to very different destinations. It became clear to Michael that his career as an engineer no longer met his needs. Though engineering had originally been something he liked, it did not reflect who he was now. He recognized that by staying in his field of work he was numbing himself to experiencing life. He came to understand that if he wanted to feel energetic and enlivened again he needed to change his career.

Michael learned to clarify his current priorities and passions. He became aware that his real love was the outdoors. He discovered that he wanted to find work outdoors that was meaningful to him and assisted others in their growth. With patience, dedication to his new vision, and an ongoing use of the empowerment tools, Michael did two things within the next year. He left his engineering job and he began working as an Outward Bound instructor, leading men and women on wilderness vision quests. He now had the passion and meaning he was looking for in his work.

Fran grew up with a mother who regularly let her know that she wished that Fran had never been born. Fran felt hurt, angry toward her mother, and sorry for herself. She had also acquired a bad allergy at a young age, which she felt was somehow connected to this situation. As she embarked on the empowerment journey, Fran faced a double-edged challenge: She needed to heal her relationship with her mother and overcome her own cycle of feeling victimized.

She began examining her beliefs and attitudes, and saw how they had trapped her in the role of feeling helpless. Her web of beliefs looked like this: To feel like she was a lovable person, her mother had to love her. Since her mother's love for her was shaky at best, she had proof that she was not a lovable person. If she wasn't lovable, she couldn't love herself.

Fran became aware that the only way she could be free of her old self-negating beliefs was to cut herself off from her past and start loving herself. She succeeded. Fran even discovered that she could love her mother while not condoning the way her mother had treated her. By the end of these few months, her acute allergy was gone.

Miracles DO Happen!

In these stories we see people who felt a certain lack of well-being or had a desire for greater satisfaction in their lives. Can we call these stories miracles? Yes—the kind of miracles that are available to any of us who are willing to dream boldly, look honestly at ourselves, and commit to a process of self-growth.

If someone told you that what you longed for in your life could be yours, would you believe it? Before we used the methods we teach in this book we might not have believed a claim like this. However, after years of seeing the powerful results in our own lives and witnessing the remarkable achievements of others we've worked with, our answer to this question is an unqualified "Yes!"

The first questions that need to be answered on this adventure of self-discovery and self-creation are these: "Where do I want to go?" and "How will I get there?" It's time to chart your course.

Planning Your Route

A Chinese proverb says, "If you don't know where you are going, you won't know when you get there." An addendum to this is: Even if you do know where you are going, you can get there sooner and with less wear and tear if you know how to take such a journey. But this is no ordinary trip. The journey of self-discovery and self-creation is the most exciting, challenging, exhilarating, confounding journey you will ever take. It may be fraught with wrong turns and dead ends, and has been known to be quite uncomfortable at times. It also has the potential to bring you happiness, peace of mind, joy, fulfillment, freedom, and insight into your life's purpose.

We invent all kinds of reasons to explain why we don't have what we want in our lives, but by and large they boil down to two: Either

- We don't know what we want, or
- We don't know how to create it.

Throughout this book, you will continually ask yourself these two questions, which lie at the heart of the empowerment experience: "What do I want?" and "How do I create it?" The answers to these questions are what this book is dedicated to helping you achieve.

To answer these questions, you will undertake an extraordinary journey. Fortunately, you are not the first person to travel this path. It has been navigated by many fellow travelers. And to assist you in reaping the greatest benefit from your journey, you will be accompanied by two seasoned guides: us. We will offer you insights gained from guiding many to their destinations.

John Steinbeck said, "We don't take a trip. A trip takes us." The person who returns from a true journey is never the same person as the one who departs. The returning traveler has new insight, new perspective, and new richness of being. Life and self are seen with deeper wisdom and compassion.

We'll begin by giving you an overview of the inner adventures that lie in store. The journey of empowerment, like all trips, has three distinct stages: getting ready, traveling, and returning home. A successful trip requires proper preparation, a good itinerary, and a way to meaningfully integrate the experience into subsequent everyday life.

GETTING READY
Being in Shape
If you get yourself in shape prior to a journey, you can benefit from and enjoy it more. The first part of getting ready is to make sure you're

well-conditioned for the trip. On the empowerment journey, being in shape means both learning how to use your mind to create what you want for your life and developing the personal power to sustain your growth over time. With this preparation, you will be in an excellent position to profit from your inner adventure.

Taking Stock

Before leaving on a long trip, it's important for you to take stock of important things and put them in order. The second part of your preparation involves taking stock of the way you view yourself and the world around you.

These views form your core belief structure. If these beliefs are healthy, you have the optimum environment for growth. If they are unhealthy, they can sabotage your ability to grow. As you take stock before your journey of empowerment, you will acquire the fundamental self-knowledge to build a healthy core belief structure. With this done, you are ready to begin your travels.

TRAVELING

Your travel itinerary has seven legs, and this is where the action really starts. Each leg takes you deep into a vital aspect of your life, where you will work to discover and create what it is that you most desire. The seven legs you will travel are:

- Emotions
- Relationships
- Sexuality
- Body
- Money
- Work
- Spirituality

In each of these areas of life, you will follow four steps—what we call the empowerment methodology.

1. *Awareness:* Gather information to help you learn about what is truly important and meaningful to you.

2. *Vision:* Translate this awareness into a compelling vision of possibility.
3. *Transformation:* Identify and transform the limiting beliefs that inevitably arise when creating something new and, if needed, adjust the vision to make sure it is believable.
4. *Growth:* Work with the subtle skills of directed thought—affirmation and visualization—to build the new belief system and the next developmental step in manifesting your vision.

RETURNING HOME

If you diligently do the exercises in this book, by the end of this inner adventure you will have new visions for each part of your life, along with the means to manifest them. This will testify to your commitment to living your full potential as a human being. In this last stage, your return home, you will learn the most effective ways to continue this personal growth over time.

How to Use This Book

This book is divided into three sections, which correspond to the three stages of the journey noted above. The chapters in each section contain concepts, principles, and ideas to help you discover your next level of growth in each area, as well as exercises and activities designed to bring that understanding into your everyday life. Each chapter builds sequentially on the knowledge and skills developed in the previous chapters, so it's important to follow the road map that's been developed for you. By following this map, you will comprehensively cover all aspects of your life.

The exercises and techniques you will be working with are highly effective. They've been used with great success by the many people who have participated in our Empowerment Workshop. They will be successful for you, too, if you take the time to do them. We get out of life what we put into it. What better investment can you make than taking the time to make your life all that you want it to be?

Many of the exercises ask you to respond by writing and, occasionally, drawing something. Expressing your responses on paper will help you immeasurably in gaining insight. You can either do this right in the book or use a personal journal to record your thoughts and observations. This journal will serve as a log of your inner travels and, as you will soon discover, become a very close companion to you on your journey. Many people like to get a special journal for this use.

We hope you will find this book useful at every stage of your growth. It was written to be used a second, third, or fourth time, as an integral part of your personal growth path. Turn to it regularly and it will serve you well.

The Growing Edge: Your Spiritual Compass

Your experience of this journey is deeply connected with the way you view the growing process. Your attitude can either nourish or encourage your growth, allowing it to be a lively adventure, or undermine and sabotage it, making it an ordeal through which you nobly suffer. As you prepare for this journey of self-growth, it's very important for you to orient yourself properly. The notion of the *growing edge* will help you here. It will serve as a spiritual compass, aiding you in navigating the bends and turns that are part of the growing process.

The idea of the growing edge came to us as we observed the way things grow in the earth. A seed—planted in the ground, pushing up through the earth, overcoming whatever obstacles are in the way, first becoming a bud, and then bursting into full bloom—is nothing short of a miracle. The new growth that has just pushed into the light of day for the first time is the plant's growing edge. It is that soft new edge of life that is just becoming.

This natural process contains a universal truth that applies equally well to human beings. Like nature, human beings, who are vital and alive, are always growing. Those parts of ourselves where this new growth is occurring are our growing edges. They are the places within us that are just seeing the light of day for the first time. In each of the different parts of your life, you will be discovering and cultivating your new edges.

While your growing edges may be different from those of someone else, we have many of them in common with others. The following are examples of a growing edge from each area of life. Whether or not you are working with this particular growing edge, it will give you a sense of what we mean by this term.

Life Area	Growing Edge
Emotions	Getting in touch with true feelings and expressing them more freely
Relationships	Committing to more authentic and honest communication
Sexuality	Experiencing more caring and trust in lovemaking
Body	Learning to love and care for it
Money	Believing that you can create greater prosperity
Work	Balancing the drive for success with a thriving personal life
Spirituality	Developing a personal spiritual path

While these examples give you a sense of several of the more common growing edges, they are just a small sampling of the wide variety of growing edges we human beings experience. Each growing edge will be experienced with any number of emotional textures.

Sometimes you encounter fear of the unknown as you move to a new place within yourself. Just as often you find a deep sense of well-being as you learn to be more alive. Sometimes you feel pain and discomfort as you move through a stuck or difficult place. At other times, there is exhilaration as you break through a barrier. Whatever the feeling, you can be sure that *if you are on your growing edge you will feel energetically engaged in life.*

As the growing edge enlivens us, it simultaneously frees us of the yoke of "should" that weighs us down. We "should" be further along. We "should" be better than we are. Each of us is unique and has different growing edges. A tree doesn't judge and condemn itself if one of its branches is not as long as those of the tree next to it. One growing edge is not better or worse than another. It is just different. Understanding that growth is a totally individual process liberates us from that all-too-pervasive human foible of judging ourselves in relation to someone else or some preconceived notion of how we should be.

To grow is to be alive, and to be on the growing edge is to experience life in its most dynamic state, that of *becoming*. With an understanding of the growing edge, you have a spiritual compass that will aid you well and with which you will become skilled as your journey unfolds.

And now it is time for your first exploration of your growing edges.

Imagining Your Journey

Before you begin this journey, let's have some fun dreaming about it a little. Prior to going on a trip, we love to pull out travel brochures, look at maps, and freely imagine what the journey might be like. Let's do some of that now. This exercise will stimulate your imagination and help you think creatively about areas of possible growth. You may come up with a preliminary itinerary of some places you will want to visit during the journey.

You will need a journal to do this exercise. (Some space has been left in case you don't have a journal or have it handy.) As you answer each of the following questions, see what comes to mind at the surface level and write that down. Then consider the question again and see if there is an answer that draws you deeper. Both the initial and subsequent responses are valid and will prove useful to you in your growth work. You may want to copy the questions into your journal so that you have them to refer to later.

Find a place to do the exercise where you will not be interrupted. Before you begin, sit quietly for a few moments so you can be in a more reflective state of mind.

EXERCISE | EXPLORING YOUR GROWING EDGES

1. What are the qualities within another that are most important to me in a relationship?

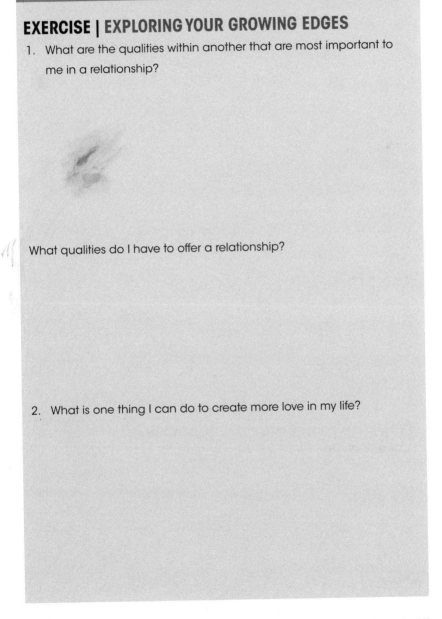

What qualities do I have to offer a relationship?

2. What is one thing I can do to create more love in my life?

More sensuality?

More passion?

3. If my body could speak to me, what would it tell me about how it's being treated?

4. If I had as much money as I wanted, what are the first five things I would do with it?

Why would I do these things?

5. If I did not have to work for money, what kind of work would I do?

Why would I choose this kind of work?

6. Which emotion do I find most easy to express?

Why is this emotion most easy to express?

Which emotion do I find most difficult to express?

Why is this emotion most difficult to express?

7. What are three things I can do to be more in touch with the wonder and mystery of life?

Crafting Reality with Thought

It's now time to embark on your journey. You'll begin by learning how to more skillfully use the inherent creative power of your mind.

Of all the knowledge pertaining to the evolution of the human condition that has come to light in this extraordinary time in which we live, none is more promising than this idea: *We make and shape our character and the conditions of our life by what we think.* By becoming adept at consciously directing your thought, you can create the life you want and take charge of your destiny.

You could spend years becoming self-aware, but in order to change anything you must become skillful in applying the principles of directed thought, otherwise known as manifestation. Self-awareness without mastery of manifestation renders awareness impotent. By the same token, knowing how to manifest without self-awareness renders life impotent. *The empowerment growth process is uniquely designed to bring these two complementary dimensions—self-awareness and manifestation—together.*

This in-depth approach will build on whatever training in manifestation you might already have, but does not depend on any prior knowledge or experience. Indeed, for some people, prior knowledge may not be an asset. They might have learned an overly simplistic approach to manifestation and become discouraged when they did not achieve the result they desired. Or they utilized these techniques effectively, but without adequate self-awareness, and manifested outcomes that were ultimately unfulfilling. Our approach to manifestation involves more than mastery of powerful techniques; it is mastery of a self-aware, conscious life.

Principles of Manifestation

"And the night was still as they were given the greatest gift that humankind can receive—the formula for having their prayers answered."

—ANONYMOUS

Knowledge of manifestation has been part of the wisdom teachings of many traditions for millennia. Today this knowledge is readily available, but because of this accessibility, people don't always recognize the potency of these principles and techniques. And if they do, they may not fully appreciate their extraordinary power until they have seen them consistently bear fruit over time. We have been working with them for our entire adult lives and hold them in awe. As we learned how to skillfully apply these principles and techniques, we discovered that not only were our prayers (otherwise known as affirmations and visualizations) answered, but our lives took on greater ease as we found ourselves living more in harmony with the universe.

We'll begin by introducing the three basic principles of manifestation so that you understand the *why* and then we'll share the techniques so that you understand the *how*. People often learn the principles without learning how to apply them. Just as often, they learn the applications but don't understand why they work. To be most effective you need to know both.

What we will be sharing with you is based on our research, personal experiences, and observations of the many people with whom we have worked over the years. Feel free to translate our ideas and language into any tradition, belief system, or way of viewing life with which you're comfortable. They all describe the operating principles of the same universe. Most importantly, use the principles and techniques in your own life and judge their effectiveness for yourself.

PRINCIPLE OF CREATIVE THOUGHT

Poet and philosopher Ralph Waldo Emerson wrote that what we think is what we create and called this principle the "law of laws." In Job it is written that "Thou shall decree a thing and it shall be established unto thee." James Allen said, "The outer conditions of a person's life will always be found to reflect their inner beliefs."

This is just a small sampling from the many who examined the nature of our human experience and reached the same conclusion: *What manifests in our life is a direct result of the thoughts that we think about each day.* If we want to change any part of our present life, we must change the beliefs that created it. And in order to create something new in our life, we must first mentally create the new belief.

At first, this sounds so easy: Why don't we all simply affirm good things in our lives and wait for them come to pass? If only life were so simple. Most of us are not conscious of our beliefs, which makes the process complex. In fact, the majority of the beliefs each of us manifest are not only unconscious, but often self-limiting.

Part of the human condition is accepting limiting beliefs without realizing how much they impact our lives. Thoughts like "I'm not good enough" or "I don't have what it takes to have [a loving relationship, prosperity, the work I want, peace of mind, etc.]" profoundly influence the shape of our individual worlds. Most of our pain, fear, and suffering are also caused by these unconscious and self-limiting beliefs.

To change these beliefs requires commitment, concentration, and courage to thoughtfully examine and alter the ways you view yourself and the world. The process of observing and transforming these limiting beliefs we call *mental clearing.*

PRINCIPLE OF MENTAL CLEARING

We can't effectively manifest a new belief if we are simultaneously holding on to an old, entrenched belief that opposes this new idea. One of the major mistakes people make when working with the manifestation principles is thinking that all they need to do is affirm what they want and it will happen. *What manifests is what we really believe, not what we would like to believe.* Until our self-limiting beliefs are made conscious and transformed, they will continue to inhibit our ability to create what we want.

Before we can create prosperity in our life, for instance, we must release our belief that we are not worthy. Before we can manifest a healthy relationship, we must clear away self-negating beliefs that say we're not good enough to be loved. Before we can realize our full potential as human beings, we must be willing to let go of our fear of failure.

Yet it is often difficult to let go of the familiar. Even when parts of our present life are causing us pain and suffering, we often still will not let go. Our present discomfort is so familiar and safe it has become our identity. Who will we be without this pain and suffering? So how do we let go? Throughout the rest of this book, you will learn specific techniques to assist you in the process of mental clearing. But the starting point is the principle of vision.

PRINCIPLE OF VISION

We are most willing to release limiting beliefs, emotional pain, and other unwanted baggage when we have a clear vision of what we will replace it with. The clearer our vision, the more we will be attracted to it, and the less hold our limiting beliefs will have on us. We are motivated to clear out the rocks, weeds, and stumps that litter a plot of land when we have a vision of the garden we wish to create. We are willing to let go of the old trapeze when we see the new one swinging toward us. We are willing to release our fear of being hurt in a relationship when we envision having a loving partner in life.

Think of yourself as a sculptor molding a creative, extraordinary, and flexible substance—thought. Your creation, which happens to be your life, will embody the ideas and pictures you hold in your mind.

Creating a vision for your life requires a willingness to explore and discover what's important to you, not somebody else. You need to ask yourself questions like these: What do I value? What are my priorities? Where does my passion lie? What gives meaning to my life? What is my purpose in life? What is my heart's desire? Asking these types of questions is one of the most creative, dynamic, and demanding undertakings in which you will ever engage.

To the degree that you have a lucid personal vision in your mind, your life will begin to change in response to it. One of the most important things you will be doing on this journey is discovering and articulating a clear vision for your life.

The Three Principles of Manifestation

Principle of Creative Thought: What manifests in our life is a result of the beliefs we hold.

Principle of Mental Clearing: To create new, life-affirming beliefs, we must first clear out the old, self-limiting beliefs.

Principle of Vision: The more compelling our vision, the more we are attracted to manifesting it and transforming any limiting beliefs standing in its way.

Techniques of Manifestation

Let's now look at the "how" of manifestation—the techniques that allow us to apply these principles.

The process of manifesting our thoughts is one of the most natural things we do. Our lives today reflect our past thinking. Our lives in the future will mirror our thinking today. In other words, consciously or not, you are already manifesting and the techniques you will be learning don't require any unusual ability. However, they do require you to be aware of where you want to direct your mental attention and to learn how to do it with skill. They also require you to use the manifestation process consciously rather than continuing to unconsciously manifest things you don't want.

Think of your mind as a piece of fertile land. Taking control of your thoughts and beliefs makes the difference between a cultivated and productive garden and a patch of wild, overgrown earth. Whether cultivated or neglected, something will grow. If you don't deliberately plant the seeds of something you want, then weeds will grow.

There are two aspects to manifesting. First, you need to create a potent mental seed, which consists of a directed thought called an *affirmation* and a specific image called a *visualization*. Second, you need to cultivate and nourish this mental seed so that it grows to fruition—this is called the *germination process*.

AFFIRMATION: THE SEED THOUGHT

An affirmation is a statement of intention describing what you want in your life. It is an articulation of the new belief you are creating. To be effective it needs to be:

Written Down

There's an enormous difference between thinking about something and actually writing it down. Putting an affirmation on paper begins the process of defining and articulating what you want. It also allows you to begin owning the possibility of this intention becoming your new reality.

Stated in the Positive

Most of us approach growth as a process of overcoming problems as opposed to creating something we want. We attempt to change something in our life that isn't working. This is usually done by negating what we don't want: "I'm no longer going to be afraid of my boss" or "I'm going to lose weight." The desired change can just as easily and with much greater power be stated in the positive: "I easily express myself when speaking with my boss" or "I am lean, healthy, and fit."

When we affirm what we don't want, we are actually putting energy into it and nourishing it with our mental attention. Instead of getting rid of it, we are bringing it more powerfully into our life. Going back to our example, we are reinforcing fear and a negative self-image every time we repeat the words "fear of my boss" or "being overweight" and associating these unpleasant conditions with our life. We then need to apply additional mental energy to negate their power. However, when you affirm positive thoughts, you immediately begin manifesting the things you desire.

One student of ours, after reframing his desire to quit smoking in the positive, wrote the following in his journal: "I did not smoke today and, for the most part, had no desire. I changed my affirmation from 'I should not smoke because it is bad for me' to 'I want to put only good things in my body.' This has made such a difference!"

Succinct

The more to the point and articulate your affirmation is, the easier it will be for you to focus on it. A common mistake is combining several related issues into one statement. This weakens the power of the affirmation, for it is much easier to concentrate on one idea at a time rather than several all at once. If you find that you have combined two or more issues in one affirmation, you should separate them into different statements.

Avoid making your affirmations wordy. Excess words are often a result of hazy thinking and may indicate that you are not yet clear about what it is you want to bring into existence. You might begin by saying "I feel lousy whenever my boss talks to me that way. I know I could come back with a good reply if only I weren't so afraid of him. I am failing to express what I am feeling, and that makes me feel worse. I know I could do so much better, and I am resolved to do better in the future."

A positive, succinct affirmation that addresses the core of this issue would be "I easily express myself when speaking with my boss." An affirmation should not be an essay. It may start out as one, but it must be whittled down to its essentials if it is to carry power. Remember, you are sculpting a single key thought.

Specific

The more specific your affirmation, the clearer the results will be in your life. A fussy and vague affirmation will manifest fussy and vague results. Many people walk around in a fog because they haven't taken the time to become clear about what is important to them. They think life will just work out, even though they've taken little or no responsibility for making that happen.

Sometimes we look for reasons to avoid being specific. You may say, "I can't be specific because I don't know what I want." If you don't know what you want, ask yourself what is important to you and focus on the specifics you do know. For example, if you want a new job, state all the details you know and the date by which you want it. "I have a great new job that is rewarding and that challenges me mentally in an outdoor environment; I'm making ___ [amount of money] a year by March 1."

Some people worry that if they are too specific they'll overlook something. The truth is that you'll never have all the information you need to make a perfect decision; some information will always be missing. Do the best you can and if you find that your first choice was not wise, learn from the experience and make a better choice next time.

For some people, being specific can be scary. It means committing to something important to you with the possibility that you may fail to achieve it. You might become disappointed, frustrated, and sad. You might create something that is not exactly what you want. You may make "mistakes." But the only way you can become practiced as a creator is through the act of creating. What comes back to you is simply feedback that helps you refine your understanding of what you value most in life and how to create it.

Again, it's important to remember that you are creating your life every time you think a thought. The only difference is that now you are doing it consciously.

Magnetic

Make your affirmation as attractive as possible. Use words that you find exciting, enlivening, and that represent your personal poetry. The more the language of the affirmation evokes deep feelings within you, the more you'll be able to put your full energy behind it.

For example, someone whose growing edge is his or her appearance might affirm, "I am well dressed and attractive." While this may be an accurate summary of his or her intention, it could be stated in a much more enlivening way: "My appearance delights me and makes me proud to be alive!" The more passion an affirmation has, the more it will command your attention and belief.

Stated As If It Already Exists

If you want your seed thought to come to fruition now, you should state it in the present tense. If you state your affirmation as something that will happen in the future, it will remain locked in the future. "I am" or "I have" acknowledges that the mental seed is planted and can now grow. "I will" or "I hope" keeps the seed dormant as a future possibility. What we hold in our thoughts is what we create, whether or not we know the means by which the manifestation will happen.

Includes You in It

Use *I*, *me*, your name, or any other method of allowing you to personally identify with the affirmation. Sometimes people make general statements, such as "The universe is abundant" when they mean, "I have an abundant life."

If you are changing conditioning you have accepted from others, it's sometimes helpful to state the affirmation in both the first and third person, saying, "I am a lovable person" and "[My name] is a lovable person." This helps deepen your belief in the affirmation.

About Changes for Yourself, Not Others

Human nature being what it is, we often look at others as the cause of the problems we have with them, instead of looking at ourselves. Given this point of view, we might say, "If only my spouse [boss, mother, father, etc.] would change, this problem would go away." More rarely do people say, "I contributed to this problem and I can change it."

The primary things we do have control over are our attitude and behavior. If you direct your affirmations to bringing about changes in yourself, you will be surprised by how much this affects your relationship with other people. The dynamic of a relationship changes as you change. You may begin to perceive that what initially seemed to be another person's problem was actually a problem created by the way you interacted with each other.

For example, you might affirm, "My relationship is steady and wonderful because my husband is learning to accept who I am."

This places responsibility squarely upon your husband's shoulders and provides you with an excuse for refusing to change yourself. We would suggest rephrasing the affirmation like this: "I take personal responsibility for creating a wonderful, caring relationship."

Someone needs to play the role of victim in order to be taken advantage of. If the person being victimized no longer chooses to be the victim, the person taking advantage must change. It's amazing to see how powerfully this works in practice. The most effective and enduring way to change a situation is to change your own attitude and behavior. Of course, this doesn't rule out speaking to and working with the other person to resolve problems.

Keeps on the Growing Edge to Avoid Sabotage

An affirmation must exist within the realm of possibility for you to fully accept it. You will subconsciously throw up resistance if your affirmation contains an unrealistically large stretch from where you are. However, there must be enough of a stretch to excite your interest in creating it.

If you have low self-esteem, you probably won't be able to believe an affirmation such as "I love myself." It contains too much of a stretch and, in all likelihood, you will subconsciously reject it. You need to back up a step and create an affirmation like this: "I am capable of loving and valuing myself." After a while, you may notice that you have grown enough to be able to accept the affirmation "I love myself."

Creating an affirmation that addresses your growing edge is an art. This is the place where the insights you have gained from your self-awareness work meet the skills you have attained in manifestation. Together these approaches create the potential for fulfilling and lasting growth. And the more we engage in this process of conscious self-creation, the better we get at it.

SUMMARY

In summary, your affirmation should be:
- Written down

- Stated in the positive
- Succinct
- Specific
- Magnetic
- Stated as if it already exists
- One that includes you in it
- About changes for yourself, not others
- Kept on the growing edge

VISUALIZATION: THE SEED IMAGE

A visualization is a mental image or picture of what you want to create in your life. Some people find that they are more attracted to images than words because an image is more emotionally appealing. Others feel more comfortable working with the words of an affirmation because words can convey an idea more specifically. Affirmation and visualization, used in tandem, create the best results. Like a movie, images and narration together have the greatest impact.

Visualization does not require special skills that only visually oriented people have. It's a process of creativity and imagination, rather than an optical technique.

In order to visualize, you need to think of an image that represents the thing that you want. If you want a house, begin to think about how you want that house to look. What style is it? Where is it located? How many rooms does it have? What is it made of? What colors is it painted?

If what you want is more intangible, such as greater peace of mind, you can build the image slowly. You can create a more peaceful image of yourself detail by detail. How does your face and body look when you are more serene? How do you physically move? Before you know it, *Voilà!* You have just sketched a mental picture.

Until you can visualize something as being possible, that thing cannot begin to manifest. You must see the possibility clearly in order to move toward it. The more clearly you can visualize what it is you want, the easier it will be for you to manifest it.

If you can *think* of an image or picture, you are capable of manifesting it. Since everyone can think of images, everyone can manifest them. If you can see them clearly in your mind's eye, all the better. Once you begin thinking in images, your ability to visualize will improve.

To have the greatest power to manifest, your visualization should:

Evoke Feeling

Persuasive TV ads evoke feelings in us that make us want to buy products. Your mental images should accomplish the same task. Your mental pictures should provoke such strong feelings of excitement that you will want those images to manifest in your life immediately. The more emotionally appealing the picture, the more enthusiasm you will have to create it.

If you want to lose weight and become more fit, create an exciting mental image of your body the way you want it. Notice the details: the way a specific garment looks, what color it is, how it feels to your touch and on your body, how healthy your body is, how proud you feel. Lo and behold, your emotions begin to build. This emotional excitement will translate into physical actions to help bring your visualized body image into real life.

Use a Single Image

Create a simple mental picture that is meaningful to you. Think of your mental picture as a billboard. Just like one depicting a scene from a movie or a snapshot capturing a particular moment in time, yours should display one strong image. If you tried to create a whole movie, your concentration would dissipate. If this billboard image is exciting enough, it will help energize your desire to create the whole movie.

If your goal is to have a romantic relationship, you might have several random images and a number of vaguely formed ideas of what that means. You might envision bicycling down a country lane with your partner, a romantic candlelight dinner, or a weekend together at the beach.

This collection of ideas, while pleasant, is not distilled enough to serve as a constant touchstone for a powerful visualization. Abstract the meaning from each one by asking yourself what feeling you are seeking through each activity. Then create a single image that contains the essence of each example. Using the images above, your single image might be during a candlelight dinner reaching across the table and touching your lover's hands while glancing into his or her eyes. Whatever the image, it should succinctly sum up the meaning of that desire for you.

Include You in the Image

You are the star of this true-to-life story, so make sure you are featured in the billboard advertisement. See yourself happily enjoying whatever it is that you have mentally created. Allow yourself to bask in the satisfaction of your accomplishment.

Be Literal or Metaphoric

Sometimes you will want to create an image that exactly replicates something you want to bring into your life; other times you may find using a metaphor more appropriate. Whichever option you choose depends on personal preference and how abstract your growth issue is.

If you are working on developing greater personal prosperity, you might create a literal mental picture—you at a twenty-four-hour ATM machine, having just punched in your code, staring at a large bank balance on the screen. If you are working on an attitude, say, a belief in an abundant universe, you might create a metaphoric mental picture—you standing in a rapidly moving stream with the water flowing toward you easily and abundantly, or you standing in a beautiful natural landscape breathing in abundant and invigorating air.

Be Physically Depicted

Like the affirmation, the act of expressing your visualization on paper helps it come physically alive. Stick figures and line drawings are totally satisfactory; this has nothing to do with artistic ability. You are the exclusive audience for this work of art and will discover, once you start, how much fun it is. The more fun it looks, the more attracted to it you will be and the sooner it can manifest. Be creative. Use colored pens and pastels to add color to your drawing.

If you aren't inclined to draw, cut pictures from magazines, use photographs, or simply describe it in words. The point is to do whatever allows the visualization to come alive for you. You might also wish to physically act out your visualization. This helps bring your visualization into your body and further enlivens it.

SUMMARY

In summary, your visualization should:
- Evoke feeling.
- Use a single image.
- Include you in the image.
- Be literal or metaphoric.
- Be physically depicted.

GERMINATION: ENERGIZING THE MENTAL SEED

A seed thought (affirmation), combined with a seed image (visualization), produces a mental seed (sometimes called a thought form). The affirmation and visualization process has literally given shape, definition, and form to a thought. This is now a potent, complete mental seed ready to grow. It now must be given energy to germinate.

To allow your mental seed to grow and bloom, you first need to create expectancy. You create whatever you expect to create. If you expect things to come your way, they come your way. If you expect things to be difficult for you, they are difficult. Henry Ford said it best with elegant simplicity: "If you think you can, you can; if you think you can't, you can't." Our world mirrors our expectations. What we believe we will have in our lives is what we create in our lives. This should sound familiar to you by now. To manifest your affirmation and visualization, you need to believe it can manifest. You must have a confident expectation, a state of knowing.

This knowing will be a breeze for some of your affirmations and visualizations. As soon as you are clear about what you want, you know you will make it happen. In these instances, the issue becomes getting a clear vision, not believing you can make the change. Some changes, however, involve long-standing, entrenched emotional patterns and limiting belief systems. The envisioned changes may seem impossible to bring about. How can you create belief in a new possibility when for so long you thought no change was possible and have empirical proof from all your failed efforts?

You start by creating an affirmation and visualization that is on your growing edge, using the methods we've just described. The effort required to get to this point builds confidence and hope—an essential first step. You may not fully believe that your affirmation and visualization will manifest, but if it is truly on your growing edge, then at least you believe it is possible. Now you must nourish this seed and let nature take its course.

The principal way to nourish your affirmation and visualization is by the simple act of repeating and visualizing it on a daily basis. This constant attention slowly and ever so surely nourishes this mental seed, until one day you find yourself accepting your affirmation and visualization as a fact in your life: You deeply believe it will manifest. *At this point, you make the major shift from hoping to knowing, and the mental seed is germinated.* Manifestation will begin.

On the pragmatic side, you will begin wholeheartedly performing the actions that will promote manifestation. You are committed to a vision you believe will manifest, so you do what it takes to make it happen.

On the less tangible side, you will begin to attract the conditions, circumstances, and people necessary to bring your vision into manifestation. This aspect is truly mysterious. Just the right person appears in your life all of a sudden. Whatever you need seems to appear by "coincidence." In all the years we have experienced this process, we never cease to be amazed by it. Although this phenomenon, sometimes called the "law of attraction," is mysterious, it is nonetheless perfectly reliable. The fact that we don't fully understand why something works doesn't stop us from being able to benefit from it.

The German writer and philosopher Johann Wolfgang von Goethe describes it this way:

> The moment one definitely commits oneself then Providence moves, too. All sorts of things occur to help that would never otherwise have occurred. A whole stream of events issues from the decision, raising in one's favor all manner of unforeseen incidents, meetings, and material assistance, which no man would have dreamed would come his way.

It is the same principle that allows a seed planted in the ground to attract all the nutrients from the soil that it needs in order to grow. Why this happens is an inexplicable mystery of nature. This holistic view of the workings of our universe is described well by the old Hermetic maxim, "As above, so below." *As soon as we firmly believe in our vision—embodied in our affirmation and visualization—we find ourselves attracting the worldly "nutrients" we need for our mental seed to grow to fruition.*

The principles and techniques outlined in this chapter will be put to regular use throughout your journey of empowerment. We hope they will be trusted friends by the time you complete this book. This is knowledge you will be able to use for the rest of your life.

Questions on Crafting Reality with Thought

Many people have asked the following questions as they begin to apply this new knowledge.

Question: How much time and effort do I need to put into my affirmation and visualization? Do I need to think about it all day long in order for it to manifest?

Answer: It is the *quality* of our mental attention, not the quantity that counts. The key to having your mental seed grow to fruition is your belief in it.

This belief is not something that requires constant repetition throughout the day. As a matter of fact, such repetition can be counterproductive, for underlying it is often the fear that your affirmation won't manifest. Remember, what manifests is what we *believe,* not what we hope for. If our fear of our affirmation not manifesting is what we think about all day, then of course it is this fear that will get energized. And that is what will manifest. If you spend just five minutes each day— before you go to sleep, or when you wake up, or while exercising—and give your full attention to knowing, affirming, and visualizing what will be in your life, you will have done enough.

It is also possible that you have created an affirmation and visualization that is so exciting that you can't help but think about it. This is fine as long as you're not thinking about it out of anxiety or fear. If we keep digging up our mental seed to see if it is sprouting yet, we get in the way of a simple and natural process. Gentle knowing and patience are qualities that best support the growing process. Nature's patience is a wonderful example to follow.

Question: If my affirmation and visualization does not manifest, what does this mean?

Answer: It means that you need to examine the process you went through in conceiving it. Some of the questions you can ask yourself include:

- Am I over my growing edge, and are my resistances sabotaging the growth process?
- Am I keeping myself so safe that I don't have enough motivation to create the change?
- Have I been comprehensive enough in my mental clearing or are there still deeply held limiting beliefs that run counter to my affirmation?
- Is this something I really want to put my energy behind or am I operating under someone else's belief?
- Do I possess the worldly skills necessary to manifest this vision or do I need more knowledge or experience?

- Is the climate in the world conducive to what I want to manifest or do I need to allow the seed to lie dormant for a while?

It is unusual for your first attempt to create your vision in the form that it will ultimately manifest. Your vision has to interact with the world and be seasoned by experience. For this to happen, you must put your full intention behind your vision—and then *pay attention to what happens.* You will receive internal and external feedback. This feedback is essential in helping you know whether or not your vision is on course and, if it is not, the feedback will assist you in making appropriate adjustments. *Skillfully interpreting the feedback we receive is a core skill for successful manifestation.*

Manifesting a vision is an organic process of adaptation. A seed planted in the ground automatically adjusts as it interacts with rocks, roots, poor growing conditions, and so on. This way of growth and manifestation is no different for us. As we interact with the feedback we receive externally and internally, we need to be able to adjust our vision accordingly.

One of our students, Beth, spent some time attempting to manifest her vision and was unsuccessful. She thought she wanted to get married, yet none of her relationships lasted. She came to us just when she was nearly ready to consider herself a failure and give up hope of ever being able to create an enduring relationship with a man.

After some exploration, she discovered that her real passion wasn't about getting married; that was her mother's belief, not hers. What Beth wanted was to experience life more fully before settling into a long-term relationship.

Beth wasn't motivated strongly enough to energize her affirmation and visualization because she had accepted someone else's dream unconsciously. Beth's attention to the feedback she got (no relationship that lasted) allowed her to adjust her vision to find out what *she* wanted in a relationship and create relationships without the pressure of needing them to lead to marriage. This allowed her to be much happier in these relationships because they were appropriate for where she was at this point in her life.

Don't give up after the first try and tell yourself that you "don't know how to do this," or say that "this doesn't work." Notice what happens and use the feedback as an opportunity for self-discovery. Learn from it and recraft your vision, based on what you have learned.

The manifestation process will mirror your internal process perfectly; it can't be any other way. If you use the feedback you receive wisely, it will offer you the choice fruits of self-discovery and self-creation.

Question: How does the idea of crafting my reality through my thinking fit with the concept of going with the flow?

Answer: We can't avoid creating our own reality; each time we think a thought we are creating it. Every belief we hold is shaping what we experience in our life. The process of noticing what we think and believe is the process of becoming conscious.

If by "going with the flow" you mean not making any choices or decisions and letting be what will be, then you are abdicating your ability to function as a conscious human being. You are using "being in the flow" as an excuse for being asleep at the wheel. You are also misinterpreting the Taoist concept of being in the flow.

To be "in the flow" is to be in harmony with the universe. It is possible to experience an active relationship with the universe, but it requires conscious intention and skill to step into its flow. Like riding the crest of a wave, you need to actively work toward mastering its rhythms. If you want to achieve this, you will need to take responsibility for creating it, because it will not happen on its own. What often happens when someone says that he is "in the flow," is that his mind becomes a mishmash of the unconscious beliefs he picks up as he floats along. Like a twig on a river, he is constantly bumped around and never finds his way.

Remember, your thoughts are always creating your reality—*it's up to you to take charge of your thoughts and consciously create a reality that is fulfilling to you.* The alternative is a reality that is unconscious and haphazard. It's always your choice.

Question: Am I responsible for creating what happens to me in my life?

Answer: If we accept the basic premise that our thoughts create our reality, it means that we need to take responsibility for creating all of our reality—the parts we like *and the parts we don't like.* Although it's easy to take responsibility for the good things, we would all prefer to find some outside source on which to blame our misfortunes. For many of us it is scary to take total responsibility for our lives.

A large part of this fear stems from having to look honestly at our thinking and acknowledge that one or more of our beliefs or judgments contributed to our present situation. Because our culture equates making an error with being bad, sinful, stupid, or unspiritual, our self-worth is threatened when we admit that we made an error in our thinking.

As we broaden our understanding of the way growth takes place, we begin to recognize the difficult experiences we have in our life for what they truly are—*feedback about our beliefs.*

When we understand this, we free ourselves of negative self-judgment. Our energy is available to create a new reality instead of being bound up in denying our old reality. We are now in a position to learn and grow from these experiences so that we do not have to keep repeating them. Life becomes an evolving process where we learn through trial and error; where *it's not only okay to make mistakes in our thinking, it's an inherent part of growing and being alive.*

Question: If, despite deep searching, I don't discover the belief that is causing me a difficult experience, can I still change the experience?

Answer: For any number of reasons, we may fall short as we attempt to find the belief that is at the root of a difficult experience. Sometimes it's because we need greater self-awareness; sometimes the belief is held at a very subtle level; or we may need more skill in using these tools. And sometimes we are not willing to accept that our beliefs create our experiences in life.

Although this process is easier if we know what belief caused our present situation, the lack of that knowledge does not have to be a stumbling block. Our power is in the present. If we are willing to take responsibility for what we are thinking now, we can change our future, regardless of what we thought in the past.

Personal Power

You now know how to create with thought. This is a huge step forward in creating your life as you want it. To breathe life into this knowledge, however, you need personal power. Many who want to grow and create more fulfilling lives fall short at this point. They read books and take workshops, but they haven't developed the personal power to profit from what they have learned. Their learning is primarily intellectual, and nothing really changes.

Personal power is the ability to find your own individual truth and then create your life around it. And an empowered person is one who can do this consistently over time. How do you acquire the personal power to bring this about? We'll start by looking at the qualities that make up personal power. Then we will lead you through several exercises that will help you cultivate or further develop these sources of power within yourself.

Sources of Personal Power

Before we begin, however, it is important to develop a healthy relationship with the whole notion of personal power. To discover how you currently view personal power, take a few minutes to answer these two questions in your journal or in the space provided.

1. What allows me to feel powerful in my life?

2. In what ways and in what situations do I not feel powerful?

In answering the first question, you may have discovered that the primary way you feel powerful is by *doing* things in the world: exercising, making things happen in your work, taking charge of projects around the house, making money, getting ahead in your career. For you, power is about asserting yourself in life, actively engaging in the process of creating.

Alternatively, you may have discovered that the primary way you feel powerful is by *being* in a certain way: being calm under pressure, demonstrating a sense of humor when things get difficult, being patient and understanding with another person, being in touch with and expressing your feelings, having an inner knowledge of the right thing to do. You experience power as your ability to receive the energy of a person or situation and respond appropriately to it.

Or you may have discovered that the primary way you feel powerful is in relationship to another person. You may feel powerful in exerting *power over another*—managing another person, controlling the behavior of your child, telling your spouse what to do, asserting your point of view and making sure it's the dominant one—or to *empower another*—helping another person to grow, learn, and become more powerful.

These are the three primary ways we experience power: by doing, by being, and in relationship to others. The first two comprise personal power, and when balanced, allow us to have access to the full range of our power—our active, doing, masculine power along with our receptive, being, or feminine power. Standing alone, neither of these modes gives us sufficient power to sustain our growth. We need both. We need the active mode to get started, and we need the receptive mode to sustain us through the growing process.

If the primary way you felt powerful was either over another or by empowering another, this is important feedback. In these instances, you are deriving your power from interacting with another person rather than having your power come from within yourself. When you are not interacting with another, this form of power dissipates. And while it is obviously better to empower others than to control them, you're still not in touch with sources of power that spring from within you.

You probably had no problem thinking of ways in which you do not feel powerful. This question helps many people pinpoint areas in their lives where they need to make a change, where they need to empower themselves. Many people feel powerless in some of the following areas: emotions, sex, caring for their bodies, money, work, relationships . . . as a matter of fact, all the vital areas of life come up when we think about powerlessness.

There are seven sources of power that we have found to be essential to creating and sustaining growth in our lives. You will likely feel adept at working with some of them, while others may be foreign to you.

COMMITMENT

Imagine that you have just made a breakthrough in the empowerment process. You have gained a wonderful insight into yourself and the changes you want to bring about, cleared away your limiting beliefs, and created an affirmation and visualization that's right on your growing edge. And you have a good understanding of how to nourish this affirmation and visualization on a daily basis.

What's needed now is the willingness to stay with your affirmation and visualization until it's manifested. The quality of personal power that enables this to happen is commitment. It is the active engagement of your full will and whole heart to carry your original intention through to fruition. This includes the willingness to keep peeling back layers of unconscious beliefs that form your resistances.

Commitment requires much and gives back even more. It gives us pride—the pride that comes from making good on our inner promises to ourselves. It gives us confidence—the confidence that comes from seeing that we have what it takes to embody a vision. It gives us satisfaction—the satisfaction that comes from stretching beyond ourselves and becoming more than we were before.

What is the key to developing commitment? It is having a compelling vision. You need a vision strong enough to attract you and sustain your energy when your spirit flags. There is where the empowerment methodology comes in. It enables you to create a compelling vision and an affirmation and visualization on your growing edge so you are motivated to stick with it through all the bumps along the way.

DISCIPLINE

What happens after we commit to affirming and visualizing the vision we want to bring into our life? What can we do on a daily basis? We develop the practice of discipline. We set up a time and a place to do our mental practice each morning or evening. In between these times, during the day, we stay aware. When old self-negating thoughts come into our mind, we do not allow them to hang around. We deliberately replace them with self-affirming thoughts.

Discipline is the hands-on aspect of commitment; it's the daily dedication to our vision. It is rhythm with a purpose.

Discipline is a struggle when we attempt to apply it without a compelling vision. And discipline for discipline's sake is pure drudgery. Athletic coaches, teachers, parents, and others often misunderstand this very important source of power. Discipline employed to build character, toughen, or punish is negative motivation, which will often, in the long run, produce the opposite of what we intend. Negating what you don't want energizes and manifests it. What we think about we create.

A compelling vision naturally brings about commitment. Commitment naturally brings about discipline. If our discipline starts to waver, we need to recommit to our vision. This is the secret of true discipline.

SUPPORT SYSTEM

We may have an excellent sense of commitment and discipline, yet still find ourselves slacking off. To keep up our motivation, we need something else. That something else is a personal growth support system.

A support system is composed of friendships and relationships dedicated to helping us grow. It can include professionals (like a therapist or mentor), close friends, and various types of support groups.

The critical factor in a support system is that the stated objective of the interactions is personal growth. There are many friendships or groups that are not explicitly intended to help us grow. These are fine. But we should not misunderstand their nature.

You also need to recognize that some relationships actually hold back your growth. These people may be afraid of self-discovery and this may prevent them from supporting your growth. Their approach to growing may be dogmatic and they attempt to force their path on you. They may be self-destructive and their negativity may shut you down. If you have these kinds of influences in your life, it's all the more important that you seek out a personal growth support system. It's also important for you to directly address nonsupportive people, especially if they are close to you, letting them know that their negativity is having a deleterious impact on your personal growth, and change the situation.

It requires effort and a clear intention to seek out and build a support system. It often takes several attempts before you put in place the kind of support system you want. Once you have a support system in place, it requires commitment to keep it alive and vital. It's easy to get caught up in the endless busyness of life and neglect your support system. Of course, there may be a time when it's appropriate to let go of some aspect of your support system if it's no longer serving you and you've grown beyond it. You know whether or not you've outgrown it by asking yourself one simple question: Am I growing as a result of being in this group?

Another important kind of support is our physical environment. Our environments at home and at work are constantly affecting us. The sense of order, aesthetics or lack thereof, noises, and so forth all influence our internal state. We can create an environment that offers us calm, joy, inspiration, or any other quality we feel will enhance our growth, but this requires a clear intention.

INNER GUIDANCE

How do we get answers to questions like these: Is this group helping me grow? What's my growing edge? What fears or limiting beliefs are blocking me? We get these answers from our inner guidance, which has many names, including intuition, hunches, and gut feelings.

To become more self-aware, it is essential to be able to draw answers from within. Inner guidance is like the fine-focus setting on a pair of binoculars. A small correction is often the difference between seeing and not seeing or between a vision manifesting or languishing. Inner guidance provides the fine focus in our lives. The more adept we are at this process, the easier our growth becomes. And it is simple— it's just a matter of doing it.

There are four steps that we have found helpful in accessing our inner guidance:

1. *Get still.* First we need to turn off the chatter in our mind. This mental chatter is like the static on a radio—it interferes with our ability to hear anything significant. A few deep breaths can usually quiet the mind. If the issue you are attempting to receive inner guidance on is of a deeper nature, several minutes of meditation on a calming image, such as a peaceful lake, will help.

2. *Ask.* If we want information, we need to ask for it; it doesn't just come. We need to turn on the radio if we want to hear music. The more precisely we ask the question, the clearer the answer we will receive.

3. *Trust.* Many times people get very clear inner guidance, but they discount it. They don't believe in their intuition or trust their own internal knowing. To prove its validity, we must trust the inner guidance we get.

4. *Act.* To demonstrate trust in our inner guidance, we must act on it. It doesn't do us any good to know something

and not act on it. After you've followed your inner guidance, make a mental note of what happened. How did it turn out? As you experience positive results from acting on your inner guidance, you will begin to use it more. And the more you use it, the more refined it gets and the better the results you achieve.

LIGHTNESS

Although we need to be serious about our growth, if we want to sustain it over time, we can't take ourselves too seriously or we will get weighted down. We need to complement the intensity that can occur on a path of personal growth with some form of lightness. Some people do this by dancing, others like to sing, and some get together with friends in a playful way. Keeping our spirit light as we grow makes the process much easier, not to mention more enjoyable. When was the last time you had a good belly laugh?

LOVE

There are two ways to take a personal growth journey. The first is to view ourselves negatively each time we learn about parts of ourselves we need to change. The other is to view every limiting belief and growing edge we discover with gratitude for the ability it provides us to learn and grow. The former approach involves taking this journey as an act of self-negation, the later as an act of self-love.

Going on this journey as an act of self-negation, and lamenting all the parts of ourselves that are not the way we want them, is the surest way to bring our growth process to a standstill. Most of us just don't have the stamina to subject ourselves to this kind of negative self-criticism and abuse over the long haul. We would rather just not look. And as our enthusiasm wanes, we move forward in fits and starts and eventually we simply stop.

When we pursue our journey of personal growth as an act of self-love, on the other hand, we are best able to sustain it over time. We gain energy from each self-discovery. We grow in enthusiasm each time we recognize our power to shape our future. We are animated by the opportunity to take on new growing edges that can improve our lives.

FINDING YOUR OWN TRUTH

This source of personal power is the most central to our definition of empowerment. Every one of us is a unique being with particular gifts, strengths, needs, lessons to learn, challenges to overcome, and contributions to make to the world. Our primary aspiration should be the discovery and creation of a life based on this composite of our uniqueness.

Yet it isn't easy to break out of the strong enculturation of expecting someone out there—the expert—to tell us the truth. We expect the doctor, the attorney, the pundit, the politician, the priest, the guru, or the therapist to give us the answer. In our fast-food culture, we aren't encouraged to take the time to know who we are and discover what's important to us. We have become estranged from ourselves and one of our greatest sources of personal power—our unique inner truth.

Finding our own truth allows us to have a strong foundation on which to build. It gives us insight into our values, which helps us make wise decisions for our life. It gives us a solid identity from which we can develop a well-founded opinion. It gives us criteria for how we want to grow . . . and much more.

Your own truth must be the guiding force for creating your life as you want it. And no one but you can know that truth. Almost every exercise in this book will help you discover and create your truth.

❀ ❀ ❀

There you have it—seven precious sources of power that can promote your growth, if you use them. It's now time to come into deeper rapport with each of these sources of personal power. To do this, we will guide you on an inner journey. All you need to do is relax and notice the images and ideas that come to you. It is an effortless way to allow your beliefs to emerge. After the exercise, we'll help you better understand what came to you and make changes as needed.

EXERCISE | PERSONAL POWER GUIDED VISUALIZATION

Allow thirty minutes to do this exercise. You will need your journal and, if convenient, some colored markers or pastels for drawing images. Space has been left below in case you don't have your journal handy.

Find a quiet place where you will be undisturbed, sit in a comfortable chair, and, if handy, put on some relaxing music. The guided visualization is divided into seven sections, one for each source of power. At certain points you will be guided to pause and close your eyes so you can more easily visualize and then draw or record in your journal what comes to you.

As you are writing or drawing in your journal, it is helpful to keep your eyes half-closed. We call this *soft eyes;* it allows you to move more easily back and forth between the imaginative and ordinary states of mind.

1. Imagine yourself walking through a sunlit forest. You walk farther and farther into this forest until you come to a clearing where you see a magical palace. You walk up to the palace and enter through the main gateway, where you see many doors, each of a different color and shape. Pause for a moment to visualize this.

    The first door you come to has *Commitment* written on it. Open this door and enter the room of Commitment. In your imagination begin exploring the room of Commitment. What do you see—what images, colors, shapes, or people? What do you hear—what sounds, words, or music? And what do you feel—what emotions and sensations?

    Pause to explore this room, then record in your journal the images, sounds, or feelings you discover. As you record your experiences in your journal, keep your eyes soft as you move in and out of your imagination.

2. Now see yourself leaving the room of Commitment and closing the door behind you. You are back to the place in the palace with all the doors of different colors and shapes. This time you come to the door marked *Discipline*. Open this door and enter the room of Discipline. In your imagination, begin to explore the room of Discipline. What do you see—what images, colors, shapes, or people? What do you hear—what sounds, words, or music? And what do you feel—emotions and sensations?

Close your eyes and explore this room. Then, with soft eyes, record in your journal the images, words, or feelings you discover.

3. Visualize yourself leaving the room of Discipline and closing the door behind you. Again you come back to the place in the palace where there are many doors of different colors and shapes. This time you come to the door marked *Support System*. Open this door and enter the Support System room. In your imagination begin to explore the room. What do you see? What do you hear? What do you feel?

   Close your eyes and explore this room, then, with soft eyes, record in your journal the images, words, or feelings you discover.

4. See yourself leaving the Support System room and closing the door behind you. Return to the place in the palace where there are many doors of different colors and shapes. This time you come to the door called *Inner Guidance*. Open this door and enter the Inner Guidance room. What do you see, hear, and feel?

   Close your eyes and explore this room; then, with soft eyes, record in your journal any images, words, or feelings you discover.

5. Leave the Inner Guidance room and close the door behind you. Again come back to the place in the palace where there are many doors. This time you come to the door of *Lightness*. Open this door and enter the room of Lightness. What do you see, hear, and feel? Close your eyes and explore this room; then, with soft eyes, record in your journal images, words, or feelings you discover.

6. See yourself leaving the room of Lightness and closing the door behind you. Find yourself back at the place in the palace where there are many doors of different colors and shapes. This time, you choose the door called *Love*. You open this door and enter the room of Love. What do you see, hear, and feel?
Close your eyes and explore this room, and then, with soft eyes, record in your journal images, words, or feelings you discover.

7. Leave the room of Love and close the door behind you. You are back at the place in the palace where there are many doors of different colors and shapes. This time you approach the final door, the door marked *Finding Your Own Truth*. Open this door and enter the room of Your Own Truth. What do you see—images, colors, shapes, or people? What do you hear—words, sounds, or music? And what do you feel—emotions or sensations?

   Close your eyes and explore this room, and then, with soft eyes, record in your journal images, words, or feelings you discover.

See yourself leaving the room of Finding Your Own Truth and closing the door behind you. It's now time to come back. Imagine yourself passing by all the different doors and pondering your discoveries: Your Own Truth, Love, Lightness, Inner Guidance, Support System, Discipline, and Commitment. Pause.

Go back through the main gateway by which you entered the palace. Enter the forest and begin walking out. Finally, leave the forest and come back, fully present here and now.

INTERPRETING AND LEARNING FROM YOUR VISUALIZATION

You now may be asking yourself, "What do I make of what I discovered in the different rooms?" Some people do lots of drawing and others lots of writing. Some get information in a symbolic way, others in a more literal way. Some don't see or hear anything; they just get feelings. What's important to know about a guided visualization is that there is no one way it's supposed to be. We each access our subconscious mind in our own way.

As you look over what you wrote or drew in your journal, for each source of power ask yourself, "Does this suggest that I have a healthy relationship or an unhealthy relationship with this quality?" Wherever you find a healthy relationship to a source of personal power, acknowledge and affirm this strength. Draw on this quality as an asset in your growing process. Where you find an unhealthy relationship, appreciate yourself for becoming aware of it. That's the first step in any growing you do. Once we're aware of something, we can begin to make changes.

Let's now look at how some people from our Empowerment Workshop experienced this exercise.

When Judith went into her Support System room, she had a feeling of fullness and aliveness. The room was filled with people who cared for her. Her boss was smiling, and her family rushed to hug her. Other close friends in the background were waving and releasing balloons with personal messages of how wonderful they thought she was.

She wrote in her journal, "I realize that I am deeply supported in my life. People value me and are there for me when I need them. I feel very fortunate in this part of my life." Judith's support system was a source of strength she could draw upon.

Jean had this to say: "In the room of Support System, I found myself suspended on pipes, as if I were being held up by a lot of different poles. They were sticking me up quite high, so my feet didn't touch the ground. I was supported but I couldn't go anywhere. This helped me recognize the fact that, in my life, the people around me aren't really helpful in understanding who I am and what my personal work has to be. I realized that I have to get out on my own. I must redo this room."

Marcia had great difficulty even opening the door to the Support System room. When she finally got in the room, it was very blurry and she had only a vague sense of shadowy figures in the corners. Marcia felt uneasy and empty in this room. Marcia wrote in her journal, "I feel the images reflect the way I isolate myself from other people. I'm afraid of getting close to people; it's too scary for me. I don't have support because I'm afraid of intimacy."

Understanding the importance of nonjudgmental feedback, Marcia did not judge or blame herself. She saw the information as valuable input. How did she work with this input? To begin with, she was compassionate with herself. She acknowledged that this was a growing edge for her. She did not put herself down because she didn't have a support system. Instead, she began using an empowerment tool that was created specifically for this exercise—becoming an interior designer and redecorating her room.

BEING YOUR OWN INTERIOR DESIGNER

In all likelihood, you found some rooms that pleased or excited you, and some rooms you didn't care for at all. You may even have had a room in which you saw nothing. These experiences were feedback about your current relationship with each aspect of your personal power. This self-awareness is the first step. The next exercise will help you redecorate each room the way you want it. As you change your mental images of how that room looks, you set the stage for those changes to occur in your life.

The redecorating process is an easy and fun way to enhance your relationship to a source of personal power. Marcia began visualizing her Support System room with distinct, clear images of specific people who were on a path of growth. She saw herself interacting with these people and enjoying those interactions. She visualized herself putting up pink wallpaper with hearts. She added lots of flowers and plenty of windows with the sun shining in. She arranged the furniture so that she could talk with others more intimately. As her own interior decorator, she designed her room exactly as she needed it to help with this growing edge.

Charlie's Lightness room had no floor! He gulped and acknowledged that his life, inwardly and outwardly, was indeed much too serious. So he completely redecorated this room. First, he put in a rainbow-colored floor. He put every fun person he had ever known in his room. He took his favorite comedians and had them offering private joke sessions just for him. He played zany games with his kids. Everybody in his room was laughing.

Each day Charlie went to his Lightness room as part of his meditation, and after about two weeks of doing this a shift took place: Charlie noticed himself lightening up. He no longer felt he needed to work until eight each night. He found that he could make time to play with his kids and that it was actually fun. He discovered a new treat—taking his wife out dancing. He even started looking forward to his meditation each day, since he was now meditating on lightness. Meditation started becoming fun, as opposed to another obligation he went through to become spiritual. Charlie began enjoying his life in a way he never thought possible.

EXERCISE | REDECORATING YOUR ROOMS

1. Think back over your rooms of personal power and see which ones need to be redecorated. You may determine that some rooms are perfect just as they are, some rooms may require only new paint or wallpaper, while others may need a major overhaul. Check off on this list those rooms that need redecorating.

☐ Commitment
☐ Discipline
☐ Support System
☐ Inner Guidance
☐ Lightness
☐ Love
☐ Finding Your Own Truth

2. Use your creativity and imagination to design the interior of each room, one at a time, exactly as you wish it to be. Describe each newly redecorated room here.

3. Spend a few minutes enjoying the changes you have made in each room. Soak up the experience of how it feels to spend time there.

4. Spend a few minutes each day visiting your personal power rooms. You'll be amazed by the positive changes that begin to occur. Who said growing couldn't be fun?

Core Beliefs

The final preparation for your journey is learning about, and, where needed, transforming those beliefs that make up your core belief system. Much like a computer's operating system, which programs what it can do, your core beliefs program how you think and behave. For most people these core beliefs are unconscious and unexamined. To be in charge of your life, you must understand the core beliefs that are making you act the way you do and change those that are not enhancing your well-being.

Much of this basic mental programming comes in our childhood. We are most influenced by the beliefs our parents hold and communicate to us through their words and actions. Our beliefs are also shaped by our siblings, teachers, classmates, religion, community, life experiences, and the media.

As children, we have not developed filters that allow us to discriminate between helpful and unhelpful beliefs. Those early direct and indirect statements about ourselves and about the world penetrate deeply into our psyche. As children we uncritically accept what we are told and shown as fundamental truths, and we rarely question these "truths" in later life. Most of our actions today are determined by the beliefs we adopted at a young age.

Although this early mental programming has the most pervasive influence on our actions, our core belief structure is continuously being reshaped by coworkers, family, the media, authority figures, our particular subcultures, and more. And, unfortunately, given our culture, many of these beliefs tend to be negative and pathology-oriented.

Discovering Our Core Beliefs

So how do we uncover our core beliefs? A core belief is one that is so basic to the way we orient ourselves in life that we never stop to think about it. We simply take this belief for granted and operate automatically based on its tenets. We are so sure that "This is just who we are and the way we think" that we never stop to consider that there is a deeply held belief causing us to think the way we do. These beliefs may not directly influence the details of every decision we make during any given day, but they certainly influence the context of these decisions and impact the overall direction in which they lead us. They are fundamental to the way we conduct our life.

Working with many people has led us to identify five core beliefs that fundamentally affect our attitudes and behaviors. The major personal growth issues that people face stem from these five categories of beliefs. Because they are so much a part of our lives, all of us have a relationship to these beliefs, albeit in most cases unconsciously.

These core beliefs are like the soil in a garden. If the soil is fertile, you can plant seeds in it and they will grow. But if the soil is not fertile, you can have the very best seeds and they still won't germinate. As we've said, your visions for your life, embodied in the form of affirmations and visualizations, are the mental seeds you will be planting on this journey. The work ahead of you in this chapter is enriching your mental soil—your core belief system—so that it is fertile for growth.

We'll begin by describing the five categories of core beliefs and then invite you to perform an "inner soil test" to determine where you need to fertilize your mental soil. As we describe these beliefs, you may find yourself being self-critical. If this happens, remember that these beliefs are so basic to the human experience that they can be considered our core curriculum. That is, they are so fundamental to living on this planet that all of us will always be addressing them at some level.

SELF-RESPONSIBILITY

When something doesn't work out the way you want it to, what do you say to yourself? When a misfortune occurs in your life, how do you respond? When someone does something that you don't like, what do you think to yourself?

One internal dialogue might run like this: "Why does this always happen to me? I seem to have the worst luck. He screwed me. I wish my life were like so-and-so's, then things would be so much better," and endless variations on this theme.

Taking this stance makes us victims of a life experience and, to a greater or lesser degree, powerless. We are unwilling to take responsibility for the experience. We attempt to place blame on something or someone outside ourselves. We become a victim.

Another internal dialogue might be: "I feel terrible, and it hurts. What can I learn from this experience? Let me pick up the pieces, learn what I can, and I'll become a better person as a result of this." There are many variations on this theme, too.

When we take this stance, we make a different choice. We accept what has happened. We don't deny the pain, sadness, or misfortune, yet at the same time we attempt to learn, grow, and profit from the experience. We take responsibility for our experience. One stance is life-negating, the other life-affirming. We always have a choice as to how we are going to respond to any life experience.

Looking at this category of core beliefs from a broader point of view, imagine life as a big classroom where we each come to learn different lessons that help us evolve as human beings. Some of the classes are fun and joyous; some are extremely challenging and downright painful.

If we have a class in our life, it's for a reason. We need to take responsibility to attend it and learn the lesson it has to teach us. As soon as we learn it, we get to graduate. If and when we find ourselves in a similar situation, we now know what to do and handle it with ease and grace.

SELF-ESTEEM

Do you feel confident in your abilities? Do you believe you have what it takes to be successful in life? Do you feel that you are a lovable person? Do you believe you are worthy of all life has to offer?

Most of us grow up with people criticizing us, and this negatively affects how we feel about ourselves. Grades, physical appearance, intelligence, athletic prowess, and social skills are some of the more common barometers on which we are negatively judged. These criticisms often damage our young and fragile egos. If we are not affirmed, loved, accepted for who we are, and taught how to develop our abilities, we are going to have self-esteem issues to sort out as adults. Since many of us have not had consistently positive upbringings, we often find areas in our life where we have a negative self-image when we look honestly at ourselves.

You may discover that you have high self-esteem in your work, but in relationships you feel like a flop. You may feel wonderful about your spirituality, but lousy about your body. You may take pleasure in yourself as a lover, but put yourself down because you can't earn enough money. If you have any of these self-negating attitudes and you don't change them, they will undermine you in those areas of your life. By the way, welcome to the human condition!

TRUST IN THE UNIVERSE

Do you believe you are part of a larger universe that is supportive and benevolent? Do you believe that there is a higher intelligence in the universe that cares for your well-being and to which you can turn in times of need? How you answer these questions has a powerful influence on how you orient your life.

People who trust the universe feel supported in life and act with a sense of security. They are willing to take more risks because they feel part of the very breath of life. They know that if they fall they will be caught. They are not gripped by fear, and this gives them a feeling of inner peace. This larger context creates buoyancy in their lives.

For those who don't trust the universe, the picture is quite different. They're in life totally by themselves. Because they consider the universe untrustworthy, they must continually protect themselves against those who might take advantage of them. They move through life with caution, fear, and inner loneliness. They don't feel supported.

Some of us have this trust, some of us don't. It has nothing to do with whether we've read spiritual books or are loving people. It transcends ideas and even the kindest heart. It is out of the domain of religious teaching. We can't be told to trust and expect that this sense of trust will somehow magically appear. Trust comes from a place deep inside. We can, however, cultivate or deepen this attitude of trust if we desire, for it is like any other belief—available to everyone.

POSITIVE ATTITUDE

Do you look at a half-filled glass of water and see it as being half-full or half-empty? Do you see life as a problem to be overcome or as an opportunity to be experienced? When something difficult happens to you, is your first response to look for the positive or the negative in that situation?

A positive attitude is not about putting your head in the sand and attempting to say that everything is great when it isn't. It has nothing to do with having a Pollyanna attitude and refusing to face reality. Instead, a positive attitude means looking reality straight in the eye and seeing what can be constructively created from each situation you encounter. It requires courage and strength of mind to unflinchingly face the truth and, amid the many paradoxes of life, find the good, the valuable, the noble.

Unfortunately, many people find it difficult to hold a positive charge as they encounter challenges in their life and in the world around them. They find it much easier to give in and give up on their life and people in general. Even more sad, in the name of being sophisticated, many people fall victim to cynicism. For them nothing ever has to work. They affirm the least developed aspects of people and institutions. They have bought a house that's at the bottom of the mountain.

Perhaps the best argument for having a positive attitude is a very practical one. Writer Richard Keiniger writes

To have a positive mental attitude gives rise to undaunted living. To fear calamity brings one to see only the gloomy aspects of everything, and lo and behold, calamity dogs at one's heels. Bargain with life for a penny and no more than a penny will be acquired. If you unwaveringly believe and expect life to bring you love, health, and prosperity, then these blessings shall become manifest in your life; for such is the power of mental energy over the physical plane of existence. A positive attitude when one consciously uses it becomes a practical tool.

FLOWING WITH CHANGE

Many of us attempt to create security in our life by trying to keep things the same. This is a natural human tendency, but when change occurs—as it inevitably does—this approach to security causes us distress. The nature of the universe is change, so expecting our lives to stay the same is misguided at best. And those who can't adapt to change are at risk of falling ill with stress-related diseases from the constant tension of trying to hold on to the past.

Life is a moving river and we must each, in our own way, learn to flow with it. For some, those ways are spiritual; for others, they are physical or emotional. And for some people the change process is so exhilarating they seek out white water for greater challenge and excitement. Whatever your approach, it is smart to become comfortable with change, because we are heading for more of it, not less.

Tilling Your Inner Soil

The following exercise will help you get a better understanding of your core beliefs. Bringing them into the light of day is the first step in being able to change those that are not serving your well-being. Check off any statements from the lists below that represent limiting beliefs you hold. Then, using these examples to prime your thinking, answer the questions that follow. For your answers to be most useful to you, think of responses for each of the relevant life areas. Just to remind you, they are:

- Emotions
- Relationships
- Sexuality
- Money
- Work
- Body
- Spirituality

EXERCISE | SELF-RESPONSIBILITY: LIMITING BELIEFS

- ❑ I'm a victim of forces beyond my control.
- ❑ I don't have the power to change my situation.
- ❑ I am helpless.
- ❑ I don't know how to deal with difficult situations.
- ❑ I am confused and don't know what to do.
- ❑ I can't change my life; I've got bad karma.
- ❑ It's my parents' fault that my life is messed up.
- ❑ I'm always the one who gets the raw end of the deal.
- ❑ If I buck the status quo, something bad will happen to me.

Now ask yourself: How willing am I to take responsibility for the experiences, both easy and difficult, that I have in my life? Explain how this plays out in daily life. What can I do to take more responsibility for my life?

Self-Esteem: Limiting Beliefs

- ❏ I'm not good enough.
- ❏ I'm not lovable.
- ❏ I'm not worthy.
- ❏ I'm not capable.
- ❏ I'm not confident.
- ❏ I'm not smart enough.
- ❏ I'm not attractive enough.
- ❏ I don't have what it takes to be successful.
- ❏ I don't deserve prosperity, a loving relationship, etc.

Ask yourself: How much do I believe in myself? How does this manifest in my daily life? What can I do to believe in myself more?

Trusting the Universe: Limiting Beliefs

- ❏ I don't believe that there is a benevolent universe.
- ❏ I don't believe there is a God or higher intelligence.
- ❏ There is no safety net in life to catch me if I fall.
- ❏ The world is not a safe place.
- ❏ I am not willing to give up control to something larger than myself.
- ❏ If I trust, I will be let down.
- ❏ If I trust, I will be hurt.
- ❏ People will rip me off if I don't constantly protect myself.
- ❏ I don't know how to let go and trust.

Ask yourself: How much do I believe the universe (God, universal intelligence, or whatever concept you choose) supports me? How does this affect my daily life? What can I do to develop more trust in a supportive universe?

Positive Attitude: Limiting Beliefs

- ❑ Life is a struggle.
- ❑ My fate in life is to suffer.
- ❑ Something bad always happens to me.
- ❑ It'll never work.
- ❑ It can't be done.
- ❑ I will never succeed in life.
- ❑ I am a failure.
- ❑ I am just a drop in the bucket, so why bother to change anything?
- ❑ The world is a hopeless mess; nothing I do will make a difference.

Ask yourself: Is my mental attitude toward life predominantly positive or negative? How does this manifest in my daily life? How can I cultivate a more positive mental attitude?

Flowing with Change: Limiting Beliefs

❑ Change will overwhelm me.

❑ Change is unsafe.

❑ Change will hurt me.

❑ Change is difficult.

❑ I won't be able to cope with change.

❑ Unexpected change will be disruptive.

❑ I need to be in constant control in my life to feel secure.

❑ What I can't control won't turn out right.

❑ It is better to stay with the known, even though it is bad, than risk something new, which could be even worse.

Ask yourself: In what areas of my life do I find it difficult to flow with change? What can I do to flow with change more easily?

Nourishing Your Inner Soil

The information you gained from the Inner Soil Test should give you insight into the current state of your core beliefs. Here are reflections from two participants in our workshop who went through this exercise.

The issue of trust drew the following comments from Nancy:

"Sometimes I am utterly without trust in the universe. I am empty. Other times, I am absolutely in touch with being in God and of God.

"When I'm in one of these places, I can't believe the other one exists, and I think, 'Oh, that other one's never going to come back.' When I'm in the presence of God, I think, 'You've finally got it. You're never going to be in doubt again.' But then I get empty again, and when I'm empty, I'm empty like a washed-out rag. Sometimes these two feelings come within moments of each other."

"I'm learning to be fully in each of them when they are there. That's the challenge for me, to just say, 'This is the way I am right now' and accept that."

Greg discovered the following attitudes about change: "In the past year I've been very much embracing and flowing with changes that life has been presenting to me. This is the result of a transformation I experienced a year ago when my thirteen-year-old nephew died. It was difficult to accept that no matter how good we were, no matter how loving we were, he was still going to die. But although for him there was no future, he did have his thirteen years and he lived life fully in his way.

"I learned from him. I realized that if I don't live my life today, fully, day by day, I'm not living it at all. I will die with it undone. This has made me willing to take risks, to just be out there experiencing what comes."

Now it's time to add the nutrients necessary to nourish your mental soil. This involves using the Inner Soil Test to identify your growing edges and then translating this self-awareness into affirmations and visualizations for the core beliefs you wish to address. To assist you in this process, look over the following skeleton affirmations, which, with some personalizing, can serve as a foundation for your own affirmations. Put a check next to the ones that speak to you.

Self-Responsibility: Skeleton Affirmations

❑ I learn from every experience I have in my life.
❑ I take responsibility to create my life.
❑ I have the power to change my life.
❑ I make the choice to grow.
❑ I have created my past and I will create my future.
❑ I am the creator of my life.
❑ The infinite power of the [universe, God, universal intelligence] flows through me, helping me create my life.
❑ I use the full capacity of my mind to manifest my life as I want it.
❑ My past does not control my future—I do.
❑ I take responsibility for making the world a better place.

Self-Esteem: Skeleton Affirmations

❑ I'm a lovable person.
❑ I love and accept myself fully.
❑ I'm capable of doing anything I want.
❑ I am comfortable telling others how special I am.
❑ I know what to do and I do it.
❑ I am confident, capable, and competent.
❑ I'm worthy of all the abundance the universe has to offer.
❑ I'm worthy of love.
❑ I am deserving of a beautiful life.

Trusting the Universe: Skeleton Affirmations

❑ I trust that the universe is a benevolent place that supports me.
❑ I open myself to the universe.
❑ I step out into my life with trust.
❑ I believe in people.
❑ I trust in an abundant universe.
❑ I am loved and supported by my creator.

- ❏ God is my friend/father/mother and cares for me.
- ❏ I love playing in my home, the universe.
- ❏ I am one with the universe.
- ❏ I move through life with ease and grace.

POSITIVE ATTITUDE: SKELETON AFFIRMATIONS
- ❏ My life is what I make it.
- ❏ Life flows easily for me.
- ❏ My needs are easily met in this world of abundance.
- ❏ My life is full of opportunities to contribute meaningfully to the world.
- ❏ I succeed in whatever I put my mind to.
- ❏ It can be done.
- ❏ I will find a way.
- ❏ Every experience in my life is a learning opportunity.
- ❏ Every day I get wiser and my life gets better.
- ❏ My life is an extraordinary blessing.
- ❏ I expect nothing but the best for my life.
- ❏ I am grateful for being alive.

FLOWING WITH CHANGE: SKELETON AFFIRMATIONS
- ❏ I trust that change brings good things to my life.
- ❏ I soften around change.
- ❏ I am a student of change and learn what it has to teach.
- ❏ Everything in the universe is always changing, including my life.
- ❏ I am patient with the process of change.
- ❏ I use change as an opportunity to grow.
- ❏ I embrace change in my life.
- ❏ Change allows me to be young in heart, body, and mind.
- ❏ I am as fluid as a graceful river and flow easily with the changes in my life.

As you delve into your core beliefs, you may be tempted to create an affirmation and visualization for a specific life area, such as relationships or money. To provide a solid foundation for the work you will do later in this book, for now focus on the more general core belief level. In later chapters you will have ample opportunity to work with the specific core belief issues that pertain to the seven life areas.

Refining Your Affirmation and Visualization

To help you in crafting an affirmation and visualization for each of your core beliefs, we will share with you several examples from the Empowerment Workshop of people getting on to their growing edge. In the workshop, we ask individuals to come in front of the group, share some background on their growing-edge issue, and then state their affirmation and visualization. We then help them refine or deepen it.

LARRY

LARRY: I chose flowing with change. Instead of being open when a new person or situation comes into my life, I close down and shut myself off. This happens a lot in my work and at home as well. My visualization is me panning for gold and getting very excited as I look in the pan, even though I don't know for sure what I will get. This gives me a feeling of being open and accepting of the unexpected. My affirmation is "The unexpected are gold nuggets of opportunity."

Us: This is a wonderful image. How can you put you, Larry, in the affirmation and make the idea of "unexpected" more specific?

LARRY: I'd probably do it by seeing myself prospecting, seeking out, and finding gold nuggets. These are opportunities for me, instead of feeling that I have to duck everybody who's coming at me. I'm welcoming these golden nuggets into my life. This would be like my visualization of going and panning for gold.

Us: Great! So state it with "I."

LARRY: Every day I pan for and welcome golden nuggets of opportunity into my life.

US: How do you feel when you say that?

LARRY: I feel very positive. I feel very good—that it's possible.

US: Do you sense what a creative step you have made? You are now the adventurer in life, rather than one who tries to push away changes.

LARRY: Yeah, I feel that I can change the way I act.

US: Thanks, Larry!

KAREN

KAREN: What I want to work on is self-esteem. I have this big judge who says I'm never good enough. That in order to grow I have to be self-critical. As I began developing my affirmation, I saw myself opening a lid on a bubbling spring. It was a wellspring of goodness and love. In its bigness and depth, it could accept all my mistakes and failures. I felt really good about this, but I also felt it wasn't big enough, considering how many mistakes and failures it had to accept. Out of this, my affirmation became "There is so much bigness in me, I am the biggest of oceans and I accept all of me." My visualization was me sitting by the ocean with my eyes closed and listening to the sound of the waves. I felt the sound and rhythm going through me, with the washing waves and softness healing my heart.

US: Very colorful and vivid. You could get an audiotape of ocean sounds and play it as you are stating this affirmation and seeing your visualization. Do you need the words "There is so much bigness in me"? It seems like the phrase right after that says the same thing. The former phrase is what we call a "buffer," a little safety zone before we leap in. Why don't you try your affirmation without that phrase and see how it feels to you?

KAREN: I realized it was a little long. "I am as big as the ocean and accept all of me as I am." That is much more powerful to me.

US: Take some deep breaths and feel that you are as big as the ocean. Take that into you. Breathe it in. How do you feel?

KAREN: I feel like I am the ocean. I feel vast, capable of holding all of me.

Us: Now, Karen, what would be a gesture of acceptance? Create a physical gesture of self-acceptance and self-love.

KAREN: I feel myself rocking back and forth. Moving as the ocean sways me.

Us: You've chosen one of the most powerful symbols of healing. It would be wonderful to visit the ocean and say your affirmation at the shoreline. And do your rocking gesture while hearing the sound of the waves. It would help you imprint the new belief you are creating even more deeply into your psyche. Thanks!

RITA

RITA: My core belief issue is positive attitude. Too many times I look at things as problems. So I've decided that in all weather I'm the sun and it doesn't matter because I can shine on everything.

Us: Very powerful image. Again, as in the last example, nature oftentimes gives us the most powerful images for growth and change. When you state the affirmation, is there latitude for the days when there are a lot of clouds? We don't want the affirmation to be a setup for a very harsh judgment when you go through the normal ups and downs of life as a human being. What causes you not to have a positive attitude?

RITA: Hmm, I don't know. I think the main thing is that I don't feel that I look the way I should look. As a result of that, about ten years ago I had some cosmetic surgery. But there are scars and different things that leave me feeling weird. I can hide them and maybe that makes it easier for me to pretend, but I know they're there every day. It's something that I have to try to fight against. And I did learn that the physical isn't as important as deeper things.

Us: That's very true and profound. How do you feel now about this?

RITA: I still feel I'm inadequate and don't feel that I look the way I should. I wonder what people will think when they know what I did. I ask myself why I did this thing to myself.

Us: You are working with many things here, which means you may need more than one affirmation.

RITA: The whole chart.

Us: Yes, the whole chart. We're all working the whole chart, and it's a credit to your commitment to growing that you're willing to face all these issues. For the moment, let's choose one. During the day, what is the issue that comes into your mind most often and causes you to feel most negative? There may be a link between several, but choose one.

RITA: I would have to say it's forgiving myself for what I have done to myself.

Us: Then this is a major classroom in your life. If you can shift from concentrating on the negative to the positive here, there's a good chance you can do it in other parts of your life. What would be the words that would say that to you?

RITA: I accept my mistake in this experience I've created that many don't have a chance to learn.

Us: Rather than *mistake,* why don't you try *learning* and keep it succinct and focused on yourself instead of others?

RITA: I accept the special learning I've created for myself.

Us: This is an act of forgiveness and beyond. It is saying that you take responsibility for the way you've created your life and this is a special way that you've learned and are learning. So will this affirmation assist you during the day when you hear that negative voice in your mind?

RITA: It's a good first step. Now that I've accepted my learning, I need to deal with feeling inadequate.

Us: And that's yet another level. For now let us affirm what you've come up with, seeing it as the next step in your healing process. You are looking at a deep issue and you will be able to come at it from different perspectives throughout this journey. So read your affirmation again as you have it and give us your visualization.

RITA: I accept the special learning I've created for myself. And my visualization is me as the sun shining on myself. As I shine on myself, I feel positive about myself. I have an inner glow and feel confident and whole.

Us: Rita, you've done very courageous work to go so deep. And we know there's more work to do. Thank you so much!

These examples should have given you an opportunity to see some of the subtlety involved in getting your affirmation and visualization on to your growing edge. It's now time for you to create your own affirmation and visualization. We wish you much success in your growth.

EXERCISE | CREATING YOUR AFFIRMATION AND VISUALIZATION

1. Review Your Self-Discoveries:
   - Go back over the answers you wrote down in your Inner Soil Test.
   - Do steps 2–4 for each core belief you wish to work on.

2. Identify Your Growing Edge:
   - Go back to the limiting beliefs you checked.
   - If several of them reveal similar characteristics, choose the one that best speaks to you.
   - If none of them represent your limiting belief adequately, then state your belief in a short sentence. Knowing what you presently believe will help you to change it. Self-awareness is the first step.

3. Create Your Vision:
   - Now that you have a clear picture of the present belief that you wish to change, ask yourself: What do I want? What's possible for me?
   - Experiment with free association of words, images, or movements to help put you more in touch with your vision. See which of the skeleton affirmations you checked might help you describe your vision.

4. Craft Your Affirmation and Visualization:

- Building on your vision and/or a skeleton affirmation that describes your vision, create your new affirmation and visualization. Following is a review of the guidelines for crafting affirmations and visualizations. Make sure that yours has all these characteristics.

Affirmation:
- Write it down.
- State it in the positive.
- Be succinct.
- Be specific.
- Make it magnetic.
- State it as if it already exists.
- Include yourself in it.
- Make it about changes in yourself, not others.
- Keep it on the growing edge.

Visualization:
- Evoke feeling.
- Use a single image.
- Include yourself in the image.
- Make it literal or metaphoric.
- Physically depict it.

PART TWO

The Journey

Emotions

You're now prepared to journey through the seven areas of your life. In this first leg, you will explore that which gives color, texture, and shading to your experience of being human—your emotions. The more in touch you are with what you are feeling, the more in touch you are with your life. Since emotions pulsate through all the areas of your life, that's the perfect place to begin.

For some of us, emotions are allies and friends and we use them to connect more deeply with the currents coursing through our lives. Fear tells us something is wrong. Joy reminds us to be grateful for the miracle of life. Sorrow, love, empathy, compassion, resentment, guilt, and reverence each tell us something about what's going on inside. We listen to what we're feeling and respond accordingly. We are skillful in working with our emotions.

For others, emotions are a part of life in which we don't display much understanding or skill. We are uncomfortable with feelings. There are different reasons for this discomfort. Perhaps we live primarily in our intellect and don't know how to connect with what we're feeling. Perhaps our emotions are all locked up inside and we can't express what we're feeling. Perhaps, when we communicate what we're feeling, it comes out in destructive ways. Obviously, none of these ways of dealing with emotions is life-enhancing.

Emotion is energy in motion: e + motion. If we have difficulty in this area of life, we have not learned how to work adeptly with our energy in motion. To work with emotions skillfully requires us to be able to do three things:

- Feel what we're feeling, and express it in a healthy way—
  emotional expression.
- Change the beliefs causing emotional upsets—*belief work*.

- Let go of negative emotions we have been carrying from the past—*mental clearing*.

Optimum emotional well-being requires a partnership among all three. We'll begin by looking at emotional expression.

Emotional Expression

Our emotions are natural responses to the process of living. To be awake as a human being, each of us must learn how to listen to what we are feeling. When we're feeling sad, we need to allow ourselves to cry; when we're feeling angry, we need to allow ourselves to vent; when we're feeling joy, we need to allow ourselves to exude our jubilance. We also need to find creative ways of expressing these feelings that are not harmful to anyone else.

When a feeling comes up, it's very much like water boiling inside a kettle, it requires expression. If it has an opening, it will blow off the steam harmlessly; if it doesn't have an outlet, it will blow its top or burst at the seams. It's up to us to find healthy outlets for the energy in motion that builds up inside us, so we neither have to blow our tops nor wear away our insides.

There are a myriad of healthy ways to express what you're feeling. Which way you choose depends on the emotion and your personal style. Each of us needs to experiment to discover what works best. We'll share with you some of the ways people we've worked with learned to express their different emotions.

Judith has a special pillow, which she has fondly designated the "anger pillow." When she is upset, she lays into that pillow with a vengeance! She punches it, yells at it, and curses it. When she's done, there's no anger left—it has all been vented harmlessly into her pillow. This allows her, at a later time, to communicate with the person she's angry with in a calm way. Her only expense is the cost of a few pillows each year.

Bill uses a large conga drum to release any kind of emotional upset. He beats his drum until he's physically and emotionally spent.

When Jack is really frustrated by work or family life, he goes on a long run, and this always seems to give him fresh perspective.

Nancy uses dance the same way that Jack uses running. When she feels really anxious about something, she puts on her favorite dance music and boogies out.

Sometimes Edward feels as if he could burst with joy. For him, there's only one way to express this feeling—improvising at the piano. He goes at it until all his joy is expressed.

When June is feeling great, she loves to sing. She composes her own songs and belts them out.

Vivian knows that when she's feeling sad or depressed she needs to sit with a trusted friend or therapist to help her talk it out. She finds the sounding board of another person essential for her emotional health.

Arthur uses a different kind of sounding board: He writes what he is feeling in his journal.

These are only some of the many diverse and creative ways we can express and release our emotions. Some methods are physical, some are artistic, and others are verbal. No one method of expression is better than another. What's important is that you find a mode or several modes of expression that suit your emotional temperament. Experiment until you find what works best for you.

One cautionary note: As you become more skillful in expressing your emotions, be careful that you don't slip into indulging them. There is a fine line between a healthy, cathartic emotional expression that is healing and a release that happens too often, goes on too long, or is expressed uncontrollably. *Express what you're feeling, and then let the feeling go.*

Changing Beliefs That Cause Emotional Upset

As valuable as emotional expression is, it does not bring about any fundamental change in what causes us to get upset. To do this, we must go to the root of the upset—what we believe. This is the second part of the three-way partnership of emotional well-being. It is our beliefs that are the cause of all the emotions we feel. If we want to change the pattern that causes us to get emotionally upset, we must change our underlying beliefs.

We feel guilty because we believe we did something wrong. We feel afraid because we believe something bad will happen. How many times have you felt upset about something, but afterward found out that you didn't have all the facts, and realized how silly it was to get so upset? What you *believed* about the situation caused you to become upset. When you believed something new about the situation, the upset vanished. In both cases, it was the belief that was at the root of the emotion. To understand your emotional responses, you must understand your beliefs. *To change your emotional responses, you must change your beliefs.*

Frances, who took our Empowerment Workshop, wrote to us several months later with this story:

Recently I experienced a long, difficult depression, unlike any other I've known. First, it was a surprise. I'd been pretty continuously happy for four months running, then I became quite ill—fever, kidney trouble, bedridden—and when I came out of it, I found myself disoriented. Soon I found myself in the midst of a deep depression.

So I tried "staying with it," tracing it to the root belief causing me to be depressed. In this exploration I recognized a lot of colorful, multifaceted gems in my depression/grief/anger.

The key one concerned my belief that my work wasn't valid or could even be called work unless it was hard. You know—"work" has to be tedious and painful. Once I realized what was bothering me, I let go of that silly belief and accepted that it was my right to enjoy my work.

For the first time in my life I have become happy at my work and I still can't think of it as work! The depression has lifted, leaving me in awe of it and myself. I am sturdier and wiser for the experience.

Frances held a deep belief that her work should not be fun, and since it was, she afflicted herself with depression to compensate for that. Only by unraveling her beliefs was Frances able to heal her depression.

The process of identifying and changing beliefs that are causing you emotional turmoil far out of proportion to outside circumstance is deep inner work and requires a real commitment. Because any belief that causes a painful and inappropriate emotional response has been reinforced so many times, your mind plays that response over and over again continuously. When the button gets pushed, before you know it that same old tune starts playing, and once again you go through your emotional upset. You seem to have no control over your emotional state; you feel powerless.

This pattern is not inevitable. You can replace the old tune with a new one. You can replace the old *unconscious* response with a new *conscious* response.

CHANGING BELIEFS, CHANGING RESPONSES

The process of creating a new emotional response to a situation has five steps:

1. Identify the undesired emotional responses that have persisted for some time. Be aware of the anger, sadness, sharpness, irritation that always seems to come up when your mother/father/spouse/child/boss/employee says or does a certain thing—that is, when one of them pushes your "hot button." Your hot button is that sensitive spot in your psyche that has been pushed so often that it is on a hair trigger. You react immediately, unthinkingly, and strongly every time someone touches you there.

   For example, you could have sensitivity to a particular tone of voice your spouse adopts. When you hear that tone of voice, you erupt. You might, for instance, hate receiving phone calls while at work from your brother because you know he will waste your valuable time and distract you, yet you cannot refuse to accept his calls.

2. Use that emotional upset as a way to identify the belief that occurs when your button is pushed. This is an excellent way to bring to the surface the unconscious belief underlying the emotional response. For example:

   - I'm not lovable.
   - I'm not capable.
   - I'm not good enough.
   - I'm too busy.
   - I don't have the time.
   - It's too much trouble.
   - I don't know how to say no.
   - She won't like me.

   In the case of your brother, you might find that you have an underlying belief that you cannot say "no" to family members, no matter how outrageous their demands. Going deeper, you might find that you feel a need to always prove yourself to others, that your self-worth depends on whether your actions meet with their approval. The energy generated in your interactions with your brother can be used to prompt you to look more deeply within to discover the real causes of your reaction. Your underlying belief could thus be stated as follows: I don't believe in myself without others' approval.

3. Once you have identified the old belief that needs to be changed, *create a new one* in the form of an affirmation and visualization to play whenever your hot button gets pushed. The new belief replaces the former belief. For example:

   - I am lovable.
   - I am capable.
   - I am good enough.
   - I love my mother/father/spouse/child.

- I have time.
- I am tolerant.
- I am patient.
- I am gentle.
- I am strong.
- I am clear.

Create the affirmation and visualization of yourself responding in the exact way you would like to. If you would like to be calmer, see yourself calm. If you would like to be more tolerant, see yourself patient. If you would like to be more forthright in stating what's on your mind, see yourself clearly saying what you need to say. If you would like to have a sense of humor in the heat of the moment, see yourself telling a joke.

In the case of your brother, your affirmation might be, "I lovingly and clearly tell my brother what I feel." And your visualization might be standing up with the phone in your hand. "Taking a stand," for yourself, if you will, and issuing a reminder to yourself to keep the call short.

4. Now create a *pause* function. This is a way of giving yourself time to change songs when your button gets pushed. Some good pause devices include three deep breaths, visualizing a red stop sign, or literally walking away from the situation for a few moments.

   If you do this every time you receive a call from your brother at work, you have the opportunity to repeat your affirmation and visualization and gain perspective on the situation before you plunge in. In this case, *you* are in control of your responses, not your hot button.

   One couple used the words "chopped liver" whenever either of them had their button pushed by the other. This lightened up the situation fast and gave both of them time to pause and play their new songs.

5. *Mentally rehearse* your new techniques. See yourself in

the situation. Picture your hot button getting pushed. See yourself at that critical moment of choice—pausing. Imagine yourself putting on your new song. This rehearsal will allow you to be ready when your difficult emotional situation arises. After a while, the new song will be the most popular one in your collection and you won't need to do any more rehearsing.

This technique requires a serious commitment to staying conscious and aware in a variety of tough situations. It requires an attentive look at the habitual emotional responses in your life. Once you have become aware of the change you want to create, you need to be vigilant when you're in the thick of things. We each have a choice in every moment as to how we're going to respond. With this technique, you'll be able to respond in a life-enhancing way.

EXERCISE | HOT BUTTONS

Take some time and think about any people or situations that cause you to get upset. Then use this five-step process to change the pattern. Space has been left for you do to this exercise in case your journal is not handy. By the way, examine one hot button at a time—most of us have several!

1. What is my hot button (a recurring situation that causes you to be emotionally upset)?

2   What is my habitual response when this button is pushed?

3. What is the belief underlying that response?

4. How would I like to react? What new song would you like to create? Create this as an affirmation and visualization.

5. What is a pause device that will prevent me from becoming emotionally caught up in the same old pattern? In your mind, revisit the scene that pushes your hot button. When you get to the point where your hot button gets pushed, visualize yourself putting on your pause device.

6. Now visualize putting on your new song and playing that instead. Rehearse the whole sequence of events in your mind: the button, the response, the pause, the new song (affirmation and visualization). Rehearse it until the new song is the only song that immediately springs to mind—at which point you'll find you won't need a song at all.

Mental Clearing

The final part of creating a healthy emotional life is to *let go of the deep hurts that you have been holding on to from the past*. In order to be free and have peace of mind, we have to learn to release the anger, resentment, or bitterness we may feel toward someone who has deeply hurt us or the guilt we may feel about a past mistake.

Perhaps you gave your love to someone and he left you—your heart is broken. Perhaps someone you placed a lot of trust in took advantage of you—you feel betrayed. Maybe your parents mistreated you as you were growing up—you resent them. Perhaps you did something that proved to be a major life mistake or that hurt someone very deeply—you feel guilty.

Emotional pain is part of the human curriculum. It's not good or bad; it's just the way things are. We can't avoid it, but we don't have to spend our lives staying emotionally wounded.

Yet it's not always easy to let go of past hurts. They have become quite familiar to us. And for some of us a large part of our identity has been created out of our wounds. In the name of self-righteous indignation we have spent a lot of our precious life energy feeling angry or resentful or bitter toward someone from our past.

Unfortunately, we are the losers. We have emotionally handcuffed ourselves to those people, dragging them with us wherever we go. They are free of us, but we are bound to them. Just think of the freedom you would have if you let go and released them from your life. And if the person who needs to be released for something done in the past is you, all the more incentive to step forward into emotional freedom.

Here's how one Empowerment Workshop participant experienced the letting go process.

I wanted so badly to let go. But although intellectually I wanted it to happen, it just wasn't happening. I woke up this morning and, as I was madly writing in my journal, it finally hit me why I was hanging on to that baggage; it's all wrapped up in my sense that I have no future. I live very much day-to-day and there is a lot of question about my future. I want to hang on to the past because that's the only thing I have. Then the whole idea of mental clearing came to me, of finally being able to let it all go, and create a new future free of my emotional baggage.

LETTING GO

So how exactly do we let go? Releasing our resentment, anger, or bitterness does not mean that we condone what happened. It simply means that we're releasing the emotional hurt from our life and that we value peace of mind more than being right. Only we can make the choice to let go of old emotional baggage. Letting go is a choice we make, just as staying hurt is a choice we make. It's up to us.

Our minds like to hold on to the past. It's comfortable, safe, and familiar. To let go of the past and step into a new way of being requires inner strength and courage. By letting go, we're saying, "I'm done with this experience in my life. I'm ready and willing to move on. I now choose to be free."

The hurts we've suffered in the past can be released forever at any moment. They are stuck energy. If you wholeheartedly want to release a hurt, you can. The purpose of life is not to continually heal past wounds. As soon as we let go of the past, we can use this unstuck energy to create our future.

If you're unwilling to release a past hurt completely, release as much of it as you can. We worked with one man who had just gone through a painful divorce and didn't feel ready to let go of the anger he felt toward his ex-wife. But he also knew he didn't want to be burdened with constant emotional pain. He felt stuck.

He was a real estate entrepreneur and liked to make deals. We suggested that he cut a deal with himself and decide how much of the anger he wanted to hold on to and how much he would be willing to release. He cut a deal: He held on to 95 percent of his anger and released 5 percent. Subsequently we received two letters from him. The first said, "I've renegotiated—60 percent for me, 40 percent I let go." The next letter said, "I've cut the best deal of my life: I'm letting go of all of it."

If you've let go of a hurt and you start thinking about it again, just notice it and gently let it go again. Your mind has become used to holding on to this hurt and may periodically re-create it out of habit.

EXERCISE | GUIDED VISUALIZATION: LETTING GO

It's now time to let go of some old baggage. Before you begin this exercise, take a few minutes to reflect on these questions:

- Are you angry, resentful, or bitter toward your parents for anything?
- Do you hold childhood memories of being hurt by anybody that you still carry with you?
- Are there any past lovers or friends who hurt you and toward whom you still feel resentful?
- Do you feel angry or bitter toward a former boss, business associate, or authority figure in your life?
- Do you harbor feelings of guilt for something you did in the past?

Your work in this exercise is to identify the deep hurts from the past that you are still holding on to and release them. Allow thirty minutes. You will not need your journal. Find a quiet place where you will be undisturbed, sit in a comfortable chair, and put on some quiet music. The guided visualization is divided into different parts; when you have completed one part go on to the next.

1. Imagine a long tunnel that represents your life. Experience this as a healing tunnel and yourself as courageous and ready to be free. Notice that the tunnel starts from the present time and goes all the way back to when you were born. Close your eyes and view the tunnel of your life.

2. In your imagination take a step back into this tunnel, a step that represents the last five years of your life. In this recent past, are there any people, including yourself, toward whom you hold resentment, anger, bitterness, or guilt? Close your eyes and identify the people, deceased or alive, if there are any.

3. If there is more than one person, start with one and picture her in the healing tunnel with you. Gently begin to relate and communicate your thoughts and feelings to her. Tell her why you felt hurt. Share your feelings as fully and honestly as you can. Close your eyes and begin your communication. Let it last as long as necessary to achieve a thorough understanding.

4. Now listen as this person communicates back to you. Allow yourself to fully hear her truth. Take a deep breath and for a few moments consider both truths—hers and yours. Close your eyes and listen to her carefully.

5. Gently begin to let go of the burden of your resentment toward her or yourself. Feel your inner strength and courage. Take a deep breath and, in whatever way feels good to you, release this stuck emotional energy. As you release any bitterness or anger you are holding, notice how freeing it is and how light it makes you feel. Close your eyes and experience the release.

6. Repeat steps 3 through 5 for each person from the last five years of your life toward whom you harbor unresolved negative feelings.

7. Go back through your life tunnel at five-year intervals and repeat steps 2 through 6.

If you did this exercise wholeheartedly, you are likely to feel lighter and emotionally open. Spend some time with this feeling before you move on. Allow yourself the gift of savoring a tender moment with yourself.

Relationships

The next leg of your journey explores the territory of the heart—relating to another whom you love. This is the stuff with which poets have filled volumes. It's exciting and wondrous. It's also scary.

A loving relationship is scary because offering and receiving love from another make us vulnerable. When we allow another person into our heart, we can be rejected and that will be painful. We can be criticized and that criticism will sting. We can hurt another and it will fill us with sorrow. And the depth of inner feeling may be unfathomable with someone we love. A loving relationship takes us to the very depths of being human and demands that we grow.

What does a loving and growing couple relationship look like and how do we create it? To answer these questions, we'll draw from the many things we've learned in creating our own marriage and work partnership. We'll also draw from what we've learned by witnessing the many remarkable couples who have attended the Empowerment Workshop. Although our primary emphasis is on a committed couple relationship, what is said can, with a little adaptation, be translated to other long-term relationships.

Those of you seeking a relationship can use this chapter to clear the patterns that may have obstructed you in the past and to bring out those things in yourself that will assist you in creating a successful long-term relationship.

Guidelines for Creating a Loving, Growth-filled Relationship
THE FIRST LOVE RELATIONSHIP MUST BE WITH YOURSELF

Begin by nurturing your primary relationship—the one with yourself. You must take the time to grow and develop as an individual. You must put yourself at the top of the list of important people for whose well-being you are responsible. This doesn't mean narcissism, but rather a healthy love and appreciation for yourself translated into investing quality time in your personal growth.

The more whole you are, the more you can bring to a relationship. When you attempt to have an intimate relationship to fill in the gaps and incomplete places inside you, you are bound to become frustrated. It puts too much strain on the relationship. Taking the time to nurture yourself is an essential element in the nurturing of your couplehood.

CREATE A HIGHER PURPOSE FOR YOUR RELATIONSHIP

When you create a higher purpose for your relationship, it gives you a larger context beyond the daily joys and struggles. When things are tough or confusing, it helps to remember the purpose to which the relationship is dedicated. Some possible higher purposes to which your relationship could be committed might be: a growth or spiritual path to help each other evolve; a way to perform service in the world; to raise a conscious, loving family; to learn how to love. Describe your own higher purpose and put it into the form of an affirmation.

COMMIT TO HEART-CENTERED COMMUNICATION

This is a threefold process:
- Speak honestly of your concerns, fears, and hurts to your partner.
- Quiet your internal chatter so you can listen and deeply hear what your partner is saying to you.
- Let go gracefully of hurts and resentment.

None of this is easy, yet all of it is essential to keeping the communication channels in the relationship clear. With open channels, the love flows smoothly, offering its vitality to both people. Create the time to speak what's in your heart.

INTEGRATE THE MALE AND FEMALE ASPECTS WITHIN YOU

To create a relationship that is balanced, you both need to put forward energy—your male side—and to receive energy—your female side. You both need to be able to communicate your ideas, visions, dreams, problems, concerns, and fears, and also to listen, take in, support, nurture, and nourish one another. Both parts make up the whole of who you are and are essential for a mature relationship.

CONFRONT YOUR POWER ISSUES

Inherent in any committed relationship are times when you push against each other. You argue about whose point of view will prevail. Power confrontations are a natural and dynamic part of growth relationships. This is one of the most challenging aspects of the relationship. It demands that both people be willing to express what they want—clearly and firmly—and to confront the struggle head-on.

If either of you hides your wants out of fear of confrontation, the relationship can't grow and one person begins dominating the other. We encourage you not to resist or be ashamed of your power struggles. Let them surface. Once the issues are acknowledged, you can work on finding solutions in which you both win. Though it's difficult to accept sometimes, our differences are part of our attraction to each other. They are also a major part of how we grow and learn in a relationship.

CREATE SPACE FOR EACH INDIVIDUAL WITHIN THE RELATIONSHIP

You each need to find time to be alone and separate. Set aside time to nourish your individuality without having to consider the needs of your partner.

This time alone is essential to the health and well-being of the relationship. It's a time to connect with your own spirit. Otherwise, each one sacrifices his or her individuality to the couple relationship and both eventually will begin to resent this.

HAVE FUN

If your primary focus is "working" on the relationship, it quickly becomes tedious. Every couple needs healthy doses of joyful play, both play for its own sake and play for the sake of the relationship. The spark that attracted you to each other needs to be regularly rekindled. The romance continually needs the space and time to be renewed. The best way to do this is to create time to enjoy each other and play together.

IN TIMES OF IMPASSE, GET SUPPORT

All relationships periodically bog down over some issue. Try as you will to get unstuck, you keep spinning your wheels. This is the time to reach out and ask for help. This may mean asking a trusted couple to offer some perspective. It may mean attending a workshop. It may mean seeking counsel from a therapist.

HONOR THE CONTINUOUS PROCESS OF CHANGE

Change is inherent in any growing relationship. As each person grows, the dynamics of the relationship must change to accommodate this growth. As each person outgrows old patterns or embarks on new visions, the relationship must adjust. Outside factors, like work, family, and culture, are also continually impinging on the relationship and triggering change. To keep the relationship alive and vital, each partner must overcome the desire to keep things the way they have always been, to maintain the status quo. Successful couples stay attentive to their joint growing edges and honor change as a natural part of the relationship.

RENEW YOUR RESPECT FOR EACH OTHER

In the early stages of most relationships, we are careful to treat our partners respectfully. We listen to them carefully, don't interrupt them while they're talking, and are considerate of their feelings. As the relationship gets older, we tend to get sloppy in how we treat the person we love. We sometimes find ourselves saying and doing things that are hurtful. We expect and assume that our partner will stick around and that this gives us license to take advantage of his love and trust.

As a daily practice, think of your loved one as you would your best friend. Create an affirmation that reminds you how deeply you value your friend, an affirmation that you will always remember when you are together. Create an affirmation that will be true of the quality of your relationship a year or a decade hence.

Whenever you are with your partner, remember this affirmation. When you are tempted to let fly with your resentment or anger, think instead of the affirmation and the validation of your partner's nature that it inspires in you. Let this affirmation be an enduring symbol of the respect you have for your partner.

Embrace the Paradox

A relationship is the master teacher of paradox. The person we love the most we often hurt the most. In a very brief period, we can experience intense joy and intense pain. There are times we can't live without this person and times when we can't live with her. There are times when the relationship offers us the most profound sense of stability—and, around the next corner, utter chaos and insecurity.

These kinds of paradoxes pervade the reality of relationship. If we are to be in relationship, we need to accept and embrace them. The stronger the relationship's commitment to growth and love, the more easily it can bend when the winds blow.

Vulnerability: The Heart of a Growth Relationship

As you read through these guidelines, you probably noticed how many times honest communication came up as an essential element of a growth relationship. It is the vital fluid that nurtures and sustains a relationship.

The heart of honest communication is vulnerability. It is the willingness to share the most fragile and tender parts of yourself with another. It is the willingness to talk about your deepest fears, self-doubts, and yearnings. It takes courage to allow your innermost feelings to be seen by another. It's scary. There's no guarantee your partner won't reject you.

So why take the chance of being rejected? The answer is because it allows you to take the relationship a quantum leap forward. When you risk your heart in this way, you open yourself to love, support, and healing from another. You allow yourself to trust another human being. You allow another to enter intimately into your life. This is a profound experience and a blessing for both people. Let us share with you a story about vulnerability.

DAVID'S STORY

There was this guy named David, and he had a healthy dose of male enculturation. He was taught that you don't show anybody parts of yourself that you're not sure about. You certainly need to put your best foot forward if you're going to win the heart of a fair maiden. Then he met a fair maiden named Gail and fell madly in love with her. Fortunately for him, the feeling was mutual.

After several months of seeing each other, Gail told David, "I'm afraid that you may reject me because I'm not good enough." This surprised David, because he thought she was fantastic, everything he had ever hoped for. Gail continued to have her moments of insecurity and shared them freely with David. Every time she did that, David felt closer to Gail and respected her more for sharing her vulnerability. He also said to himself, "My God, I never would share stuff like that. If she knew I wasn't totally together, she might reject me. I'd better keep putting my best foot forward."

Meanwhile, David started having his own fears squirming around inside. Finally, after a few more months passed, during which Gail continued to freely share her deepest concerns about not being good enough for him, David worked up the courage to tell Gail that he had some fears of his own. He told her that he was afraid she might reject him for someone else. He told her that he had been rejected in a past relationship and was afraid he might get rejected again. He told her that he was head over heels in love with her and it was scary to be so out of control. Each time he shared these deep feelings, he took a breath and hoped that she wouldn't walk away.

To his surprise and utter joy, Gail responded with great caring. She acknowledged that it must have been hard for him to overcome his past conditioning and speak so vulnerably. She told him that she loved him all the more and had no intention of leaving him.

David began realizing that as he opened up his fears of rejection to Gail, her love was helping to heal them. He started feeling that not only was it safe to be vulnerable with Gail; it actually helped heal his fears. His fear that Gail would think less of him if he shared his insecurity was gone. With nothing to hide or protect, he began openly discussing and healing his other deep fears about the relationship. Eventually, the relationship moved to a place where they both felt safe at any time sharing what was really in their hearts.

As a result of their acts of vulnerability, Gail and David came away with greater acceptance of themselves and each other. They grew and the relationship flowered.

If you, too, want your most intimate relationship to grow and flourish, you must work to heal and transform the deepest fears you hold about it. The first step in this process is discovering your fears and beginning your internal healing and transformation process. The second step is being willing to share these fears with the one you love. This next exercise will be an opportunity to take that first step of discovering and healing your fears.

Healing Relationship Fears

You will soon begin healing, and transforming the deepest fears you hold about a loving, committed relationship. These are the fears that make you feel most vulnerable. Fear and vulnerability are not easy things to face, and there are all sorts of ways we can trick ourselves out of coming to terms with these issues. For that reason, we're including a list of common fears to help you get through that first mental block; then, as part of the exercise, we'll help you overcome the many resistances that may come up when you come close to expressing your vulnerability.

The first part of the exercise is a guided visualization to help you bring your fears about relationships to the surface. You then will choose the fear that is most core and come to understand it better. Then you'll be guided to transform that fear into a vision of how you would like it to be. You'll create your vision in both image and affirmation.

In the second part of the exercise, you will list any resistances you have to believing in your affirmation. This is a powerful mental clearing tool that will allow you to bring to the surface the old, unconscious mental programming, which might otherwise sabotage your affirmation.

Roberta had the following experience during this process:

After my marriage dissolved, I felt badly betrayed by someone I had really believed in. Since then I've pretty much slammed and bolted the door that leads to new relationships.

I wanted to turn this fear around. The first affirmation that I came up with was "I can have intimate, vulnerable relationships because I have discrimination and wisdom."

Going deeper into my resistances, I realized that I am not open to being hurt. Yet if I'm to be vulnerable, I have to be open to being hurt. Going deeper still, I realized that being hurt is such a devastating experience because my self-esteem is destroyed. This is why it was so painful when my marriage fell apart. I was not strong, wise, or whole.

So the final affirmation I came up with is "I rejoice in my strength, wisdom, and wholeness and allow an intimate, vulnerable relationship into my life."

Because of all the pain that went before, I can now really own these new qualities.

Common Fears

A list of common fears about relationships appears below, along with affirmations some people have found helpful in addressing those fears. These will prime the pump a bit and help you get at your own fears.

FEAR: My partner will leave me when he/she finds out who I really am.
AFFIRMATION: I affirm all of my humanity and know that the deepest way of being loved is by being fully known.

FEAR: I am not deserving of a loving relationship.
AFFIRMATION: I am a unique and totally lovable person, and deserve all the gifts of a wonderful, loving relationship.

FEAR: I won't find anyone who meets my requirements as an ideal partner.
AFFIRMATION: If God could come up with someone like me, I'm sure there's another one around who can match me. I attract that person to me.

FEAR: The person I love will leave me.
AFFIRMATION: I feel whole and complete exactly as I am and attract into my life someone committed to a long-term relationship.

FEAR: I'll be hurt if I open my heart in the relationship.
AFFIRMATION: I embrace the paradox of relationship—pain and joy. I learn from both of them.

FEAR: I will lose my independence and individuality and get trapped in a relationship.
AFFIRMATION: I choose a partner who supports my independence and individuality, and together we balance being together and being apart.

FEAR: My relationship will be just like my parents' difficult relationship.
AFFIRMATION: I create my own truth in my relationship. I am free of the past.

FEAR: My partner will be just like my mother/father.
AFFIRMATION: I heal my relationship with my mother/father and attract a partner who is appropriate for me.

FEAR: My relationship won't work out.
AFFIRMATION: I trust that I am clear enough to choose wisely and commit to keeping the relationship alive and growing.

FEAR: I will be controlled in the relationship.
AFFIRMATION: I own my own power and choose a partner who is empowering.

FEAR: My partner will not be faithful.
AFFIRMATION: I choose a partner committed to monogamy.

FEAR: My partner will be attracted to other men/women.
AFFIRMATION: I accept the attraction of my partner to other people as natural and healthy. I encourage my partner and myself to develop other friendships, and support these friendships.

FEAR: Relationships are too complex in this day and age and are doomed to fall apart.
AFFIRMATION: Relationships work when love and the willingness to grow are present. I create a loving, growing, and totally successful relationship.

EXERCISE | FROM FEAR TO VISION

Allow approximately thirty minutes to do this exercise. You will need your journal and some colored pens, colored pencils, or other drawing materials. Space has been left in case you don't have your journal handy. Find a quiet place where you will be undisturbed. Sit in a comfortable chair and put on some soft, relaxing music.

The guided visualization is divided into several parts. At certain points, you will be guided to close your eyes so you can more easily visualize. Draw or record your perceptions in your journal.

Remind yourself to maintain soft eyes as you move back and forth between your imaginative and ordinary states of mind. Get ready for this inner exploration.

1. Take a few deep breaths and feel the courage within you to explore your heart (note that *courage* comes from the Latin root *cor*, meaning "heart"). Close your eyes and visualize your courage. One way of connecting with your heart is to place a hand over your heart area.

2. Go into your heart and begin discovering those fears that you're most afraid of sharing with someone you love. Make note of the fears that apply to you. The following questions may help you.

   a. It is most difficult for me to tell someone I love that I am afraid of:

   Rejection

   Abandonment

   Betrayal

   Loss of freedom

   Loss of self

   Not being deserving of love

   b. What is it that causes you to withdraw, to pull away in your intimate love relationship?

c. What situations seem to cause these fears to crop up? Write down your observations.

3. Keep going deeper into these fears and see if there is one fear that seems to embrace the other fears, one fear that is at the core. See if a particular fear seems to be the worst. Then write down what you're afraid might happen. Record in your journal, with soft eyes, what you discover.

4. Keep going deeper into that fear. What does the fear look like? What color is it? What texture is it? What shape is it? Close your eyes and visualize and experience the fear. Using colored pens, colored pencils, or pastels, draw a picture of the fear.

5. How does looking at this fear make you feel? Write down the words that come to you. Then ask the fear two questions: Why have I created you in my life? What do you have to teach me? Reflect on these questions. Record your answers in your journal.

6. You created your fear. It is just as possible for you to create the most ideal circumstance for yourself that you can imagine. How would you like things to be? What is your vision of what lies on the other side of the fear? What does this vision look like? What image captures the feeling of this vision? What words describe how this vision allows you to feel? See yourself moving through your fear and fully becoming one with your vision. Draw the image and record the words that describe your vision.

7. Allow this vision, and all the insight you have gained from it, into your heart. Breathe in and experience this expanded feeling. Do this several times. Then translate your vision into an affirmation of how you would like your relationships to be. Write it down.

8. After you have created your affirmation, do the following mental clearing process. Clear as many layers of resistance as you can.

a. Now that you have written down your affirmation, write down any resistances you have to believing it. For example, if your core fear is rejection, your affirmation might be: "I accept myself and share who I am totally." Your resistance to believing this might be: "No way. I'll get hurt if I fully open myself to someone." Now, instead of negating the resistance, which only energizes it more by according it mental attention, reaffirm your affirmation and give it your mental energy. Once again, write down your affirmation. Then write down the next resistance that comes up for you. The next resistance that comes up might be: "Forget it. No one will love me when they really get to know me."

b. Do this three to five times. You'll discover that it's like peeling the layers of an onion. You peel off one resistance and notice another, more subtle resistance underneath. Because you are working with a deeply ingrained fear, it takes time to identify all the resistances to believing your new affirmation. Remember to reaffirm your affirmation each time you write your resistance so as not to get overwhelmed by the resistances.

c. Through this peeling process, you will either find that the affirmation is believable to you and you are capable of overcoming these resistances, or that you need to back up because you are beyond your growing edge. If you are beyond your growing edge, using the first example, perhaps the affirmation might need to be "I accept myself," leaving out the phrase "and share who I am totally." Use your resistances as feedback and adjust your affirmation accordingly.

9. Now write down your final affirmation.

Enjoy your new growth. See you on the next leg of the journey!

Sexuality

The deepest impulse we possess is our sexuality. It is a powerful and primal force. It can be used not only to bring new life into existence, but to regenerate our present life with passion and creativity. When we do not express our sexuality, our life force stagnates and our vital energies dissipate.

The full expression of our sexuality lies not in the mastery of mechanical techniques for inducing pleasure but rather in loving, intimate, sensual, sacred engagement with life. Engagement with life sees love as the gift that makes lovemaking a joyous act. Engagement with life draws out our passion and inspires us to make it happen. Engagement with life acknowledges that the divine energy that animates the universe is the same energy that animates us. Willingness to fully share our life force is the most intimate union we can experience. This is true sexuality.

We often stifle our sexuality by limiting how we define it. In our culture, sexuality is defined as the act of intercourse; for some, it gets even more narrow and is seen exclusively as the orgasm. Sam Keen speaks eloquently to this point:

> Our bodies have become erotic deserts, deprived of the multitude of sensory delights. And the genitals are assigned the role of oasis in a wasteland of pleasure. We expect the flowering of sex to make up to us for a desiccated life of the senses."

Why not expand your love life from the single arena of the bedroom to all of life? Why not allow your sexuality to become your love *for* life, so that you make love not only to your partner, but also to the mountain you climb, the flowers you arrange, the work you perform, and the spiritual quest you undertake? When defined in this fuller way, your sexuality is your passion for living the whole of your life.

Let's begin exploring your passion by going to its source—what you believe. What does sexuality look like for you?

Sexual Beliefs

As we have been saying again and again, what you believe is what you get. What do you believe about your sexuality? How much of what you believe reflects who you are today—and how much is outdated past programming?

Most of your attitudes about sexuality are unconsciously received from your parents, friends, religion, advertising, movies, past lovers, and society at large. In some cases, these beliefs reflect your true sexuality, and you should hold on to them. In other cases, you have picked up beliefs that inhibit or limit your sexual expression, beliefs that are not true of who you are today. You need to remove them; to weed your mental garden. Most of us have accumulated a surprising number of unnoticed weeds over the years.

This process of sorting out what is true for you is obviously important, yet not always easy, given the complex times we live in. The sexual revolution opened up many doors, eliminated many taboos, and presented us with a variety of sexual lifestyle options and belief systems from which to choose. People today are deciding whether to be heterosexual, homosexual, bisexual, monogamous, or celibate; whether or not to start off a relationship by discussing AIDS; whether to have a child or not to have a child. It isn't how it used to be.

The process of sorting through what you believe and what you do not believe to determine what represents your own unique truth is an extraordinarily empowering act. It is a declaration to yourself that you are willing to take complete responsibility for creating your life. Inherent in this process is asking yourself, "What do I value? What do I want?" What for one person is a limiting belief may for another be the deepest truth.

For example, one person might believe that it is important to be monogamous if you are married but not important if you are just dating or living with someone. Another person might believe that a commitment to live together is the same as marriage and thus fidelity is essential. Still someone else might believe that a person should be able to engage in lovemaking outside of these relationships.

Monogamy is just one of any number of sexual issues with persuasive arguments on all sides. We live in a time and a culture that leave us free to find our own truth. The main point is, though, that the rules we live by must truly be our own. They must reflect our deepest being. They must be expressions of who we are. If we adopt standards that come to us from someone else's value system, they will not be our own, no matter how coherent and well-intentioned they are. As we bring each of our beliefs into this kind of scrutiny, we sort out which of them are truly ours and which have been imposed by our own fears or outside agents.

The next exercise will help you identify and overcome these limitations. We'll begin by looking at a few examples of what some people have discovered as their limiting beliefs about sexuality.

EXAMPLES OF LIMITING SEXUAL BELIEFS

- Long-term relationships are fated to become sexually boring and lack passion.
- Communicating what I want takes away spontaneity in lovemaking.
- My partner will not think I am sexually attractive because my body is not nice enough.
- Having preferences as to which sexual acts I like is a sign of inhibition.
- I have been hurt in past sexual relationships and I will be hurt again if I am intimate.
- My sexual desire rhythm isn't normal.
- As a woman, if I express my sensuality, men will take it as a sexual invitation.

- As a man, I always have to initiate and perform during lovemaking.
- The only way to make love is to have an orgasm.
- I cannot enjoy sexual pleasure by myself.
- It is more important for my partner to get pleasure from sex than it is for me.

Turning Limiting Beliefs Around

Once you have identified your limiting beliefs and attitudes, the next step is to replace them with new, more expanded beliefs. These new attitudes take off your mental blinders and open up your view. We call this mental clearing technique the "turnaround" process. You take your limiting idea and expand it to include a broader perspective. Other ways to describe this process include expanding our context or reframing our ideas. *A turnaround often takes us out of either/or narrow thinking and frees up our imagination.* In becoming more open-minded, we begin to see our options in terms of both/and rather than either/or.

Some sexually limiting beliefs may weigh large in your life and emerge as the growing-edge issues you choose to work with in the exercises at the end of this chapter, while others are just weeds to remove and be done with. Following are the turnarounds created by the people whose limiting beliefs we shared above.

Turnaround Examples

LIMITING BELIEF: Long-term relationships are fated to become sexually boring and lack passion.

TURNAROUND: The level of passion and vitality in my sex life is a direct reflection of my commitment to continually opening deeper parts of myself and to my commitment to being fully passionate and alive in the rest of my life.

LIMITING BELIEF: Communicating what I want takes away my spontaneity in lovemaking.

TURNAROUND: The more I share what I want, the more fun lovemaking is for me.

LIMITING BELIEF: My partner will not think I am sexually attractive because my body is not nice enough.
TURNAROUND: I love all of myself and offer my partner my full, radiant being.

LIMITING BELIEF: Having preferences as to which sexual acts I like is a sign of inhibition.
TURNAROUND: I am unique in my sexuality, with the right to decide what I do and do not enjoy.

LIMITING BELIEF: I have been hurt in past relationships and I will be hurt again if I am intimate.
TURNAROUND: I have the wisdom and discrimination to use my past experiences to wisely create intimacy in a new relationship.

LIMITING BELIEF: My sexual desire and rhythm aren't normal.
TURNAROUND: I discover and trust my unique sexual rhythms.

LIMITING BELIEF: As a woman, if I express my sensuality, men will take it as a sexual invitation.
TURNAROUND: I make sure I am clear what message I'm projecting and my energy speaks for itself.

LIMITING BELIEF: As a man, I always have to initiate and perform in lovemaking.
TURNAROUND: I create my own standard of what gives me satisfaction.

LIMITING BELIEF: The only way to make love is to have an orgasm.
TURNAROUND: What I want from lovemaking is intimacy, deep caring, and union. Sometimes this includes orgasm.

LIMITING BELIEF: I cannot enjoy sexual pleasure by myself.
TURNAROUND: The simple passion of enjoying sexual pleasure is available to me at any time. I am the master of my own sensual/sexual enjoyment.

LIMITING BELIEF: It is more important that my partner get pleasure from lovemaking than for me.
TURNAROUND: Lovemaking is a dance of mutual pleasure and union for my partner and me. I take responsibility to offer and receive sexual pleasure.

A few parting words before you go off, mental hoe in hand, to crawl around weeding your garden:

These turnarounds are stepping-stones to creating affirmations. Their primary purpose is to clear the garden of weeds. They can be stated more loosely than an affirmation.

You may not fully believe all your turnarounds right away. It takes time. And, as you know based on all the inner work you have already done, creating a new belief causes change to start.

As you do this next exercise, pay attention to what was told or not told to you by your mother and father; notice what was communicated by religion, past friends, and lovers; think carefully about the constant barrage of messages from television and film. Notice the things that you believe about the act of lovemaking, about intimacy, sensuality, and your passion for life—how you express your life force.

In the upcoming exercise, be aware that some of your limiting beliefs will be more superficial, while others will be deep-rooted and tougher to turn around. You may also discover that you do not have a lot of weeds, that the sexuality part of your mental garden is clear. If this is the case, celebrate your clear garden and prepare to cultivate anew. Do be careful, however: Don't think your garden is clear simply because you have not thoroughly examined it.

EXERCISE | TURNAROUNDS

Allow twenty to thirty minutes to do this exercise. You will need your journal. Space has been left in case you don't have it handy.

1. Write down your limiting beliefs about sexuality. First concentrate just on your limiting beliefs and do not think about their turnarounds.

2. When you feel you have written down all the limiting beliefs that you can find, start turning them around. Start with the ones that are most important to turn around. Don't worry if you can't turn each one around perfectly; just do the best you can.

Sensuality: The Ever-Present Invitation

One of the primary ways we express our sexuality is through our sensuality.

We can experience our sexuality each time we see a bird in flight, hear a brook gurgling, smell the fragrance of a flower, taste the subtle seasoning of exotic food, or dance with the blood pulsating through our bodies. It is in these ways that our sexuality becomes an integral part of our daily life, giving us continual delight and pleasure. It is not a separate act, divorced from daily living, isolated in time, confined to a bedroom and dependent on a partner. As exquisite as the lovemaking act is, there is much more available to us as sexual beings. One of the most joyous ways we experience our aliveness is through our senses.

What an extraordinary gift we could give ourselves if each day we decided to smell one rose! Experiencing a rose is an erotic experience. The flower's physical beauty first captures the eye—the softness of its texture, the grace of its petals, the subtlety of its color. Soon the most delicate of fragrances wafts through your nostrils and you feel compelled to bring your nose right to the rose, taking in a deep breath of its perfume.

Sensual interaction with life is available to us all day long, every day of our lives. We can reawaken our senses just by knowing that they are there. We can take our involvement with life a step further by engaging our senses with creativity and passion: To dance with trees, sing with birds, and cavort with clouds is to have a sexual relationship with life. In these acts, we experience the union of our life force with the life force of all creation. We merge our individuality with the individuality of life itself.

EXERCISE | SENSUALITY

In this exercise, your job is to totally indulge your senses. You are to relive at least two of the most sensually exciting experiences you have ever had, then enhance them to make them even better. The purpose of this exercise is simply to have fun by engaging your senses as fully as possible.

To inspire your memory and imagination, here are a few snapshots of some favorite scenes:

- The feeling of running on a hot day, then cooling off in a lake

- Making love on a beach
- Climbing a mountain on a clear, crisp fall day
- Working in an herb and vegetable garden that has just come into full bloom
- Experiencing the delight of a gourmet meal under the stars
- The first-time sights, smells, sounds, and tastes of a new culture
- Skiing on freshly fallen powdered snow
- Holding a newborn baby

1. Re-create one of your favorite sensual experiences from your past in your mind, paying very close attention to what is happening to each of your senses. See, smell, touch, hear, and taste everything. Become aware of secondary sensations you may not have been paying attention to at the time. If you were seeing, imagine the sounds. If you were smelling, what were the tastes? As you get fully into the scene, feel free to embellish, exaggerate, and fantasize about how you could make it even better. Write the experience down in detail.

2. Now choose a second scene to remember and enhance. Fully engage and delight your senses. Write down your experiences.

See if you can bring sensually pleasing things into your life on a more regular basis. Reorganize your life so that sensually enjoying yourself is at least as important as carrying out all your required tasks and fulfilling your responsibilities. It's your life—have fun with it!

Lovemaking

With this fuller view of sexuality, let's not forget the lovemaking act itself. With a mental attitude that reflects your clarity, a deepened passion for life, and an awakened sensuality, you will inevitably find that lovemaking expands, too.

If lovemaking could be any way you wanted it, how would you have it be? Letting your imagination soar, what does making love to another look like? It's time to open up the range of possibility; to explore the realms of deep intimacy, sensual rapture, merger with another, the sharing of the life force, and the offering and receiving of pleasure.

As we know well, thought creates reality. Once you create the vision, you set the stage for reality to follow. The clearer your vision, the more easily it can begin to manifest. The next exercise is designed to bring images of your ideal lovemaking scene to the surface of your mind. Let go of any preconceived notions of how it should be. Let your own truth be the guiding voice. Keep your heart open, your senses alive, and your passion flowing.

EXERCISE | LOVEMAKING

Allow approximately twenty minutes to do this exercise. You will need your journal. Space has been left in case you don't have it nearby. Find a quiet place where you will be undisturbed. Sit in a comfortable chair and put on some soft, relaxing music. There are eight questions to assist you in creating your vision. Record your response after reading each question. To help you stay inward and in touch with your feelings, images, and thoughts, use soft eyes as you record your responses.

Let your sexuality freely express itself—and have a great time!

1. Begin to visualize the ideal setting or environment for your lovemaking. Where are you? What is special about the setting? Are there any things that you want to include in your setting?

2. As you are entering into your ideal lovemaking experience, how do you feel about yourself:
    a. Physically?

    b. Emotionally?

    c. Mentally?

d. Spiritually?

3. As you create this special act together, how do you feel about your partner:
   a. Physically?

   b. Emotionally?

   c. Mentally?

   d. Spiritually?

4. In your ideal vision, how is lovemaking initiated?

5. What happens in the early stages of your lovemaking experience? What words, communications, gestures, activities, and qualities make this early phase fulfilling for you?

6. As you move into the main phase of your ideal lovemaking session, what happens? What communications, gestures, activities, and qualities make this part of your experience fulfilling?

7. How do you bring closure to your lovemaking experience so that the completion is ideal?

8. Gently review the entire ideal lovemaking experience you just created and ask yourself: What made this experience meaningful for me?

Here are a few comments from people who did this exercise:

What happened for me before the lovemaking was just as important as what happened during, and it's the thing that in real life I leave out most often. We went for a walk on the beach and collected treasures and played tag and told jokes and tackled each other in the sand. This was the setup, the place for me to connect.

I went to a place where nature surrounds me, a familiar place that means a lot to me. I made love there a long time ago. What was important was that I was outside and I could commune with nature. I could feel God and nature surging through me, and in that feeling I could let everything else go.

We were in a glass room—I like the comfort of a bed and being in a warm place. The full moon was shining down on us and there was this feeling of connection with the universe. We did a dance together first, which brought an element of spiritual union that colored the lens of the lovemaking experience.

Creating an Affirmation and Visualization for Your Sexual Growing Edge

By now, you know a fair amount about your sexuality. It's time to synthesize the work you've done and focus your insights into the specific next step for growth—an affirmation and visualization that addresses your growing edge for sexuality. Here are a few actual affirmations and visualizations created by people in our Empowerment Workshop and the process they went through in creating them.

Barbara learned that her biggest limiting belief was her fear of asserting her needs while making love. She had a limiting belief that she would turn a man off if she asked for what she wanted. She learned in the lovemaking exercise that what was particularly important to her in lovemaking was to feel cared for and to feel good about herself. Building on these insights, she created this affirmation: "I love myself and ask for what I need in lovemaking." Her visualization was communicating her needs lovingly and clearly to her partner.

Richard discovered in the limiting-beliefs exercise that he had a belief that if he was not currently in a sexual relationship, his sexuality was dead. He was also clear that he was not interested in one-night stands. Using turnarounds and the sensuality exercise, he discovered that his sexuality was quite alive—it was being expressed through the passion he had for his work and his daily interaction with nature. After this self-discovery, Bill created the following affirmation: "My sexuality is passionately alive and I nourish it daily." His visualization was walking through the woods by his house with his senses fully interacting with everything around him. In this way he released the narrow definition his culture had placed on sexuality.

EXERCISE

It's time to create your own sexuality affirmation and visualization.

1. Go back and review your limiting beliefs and turnarounds, your exploration of sensuality, and your ideal lovemaking scenario.

2. Synthesize what you have learned from these exercises and then ask yourself, What is the most important next step in my sexual growth? What is my growing edge?

3. From the insight you have generated, create your affirmation and visualization. My affirmation for sexuality is:

My visualization for sexuality is:

We leave you with this insight from Shirley about the quality of her experience many months after doing these exercises:

Significance has taken on new meanings for me. What used to be so significant in my life—wanting a man to call me, needing to have something to do on Friday night, etc.—is now relatively insignificant. What used to be somewhat insignificant is now extremely significant. Is it really just lately that birds started flying above me as I drive to work? Is it really just lately that the sun has begun to rise and set so beautifully?

What is certain is that I have really begun to live life, fully and consciously.

In closing this chapter of our journey together, we hope you have drunk deeply of your passion. May your love life and your love of life be as one.

The Body

Your body is miraculous. It creates and brings forth new physical life. It allows you to experience the sensual pleasures and delights of the earth. It transports you on the planet. It gives you the opportunity to express joy through dance, movement, and play. It enables you to experience physical health and vitality. It helps define your personal identity. It allows you to express your ideas, feelings, and visions. It lets you experience the life energy that flows throughout the universe. It enables you to learn the lessons of the earth, and through them, grow and evolve. Our bodies are our sacred homes.

What images come to your mind when you think about your body? Do you have a relationship with it? How do you want your body to look, feel, perform? Do you have a vision for it? Is your body well cared for? Do you have a plan for maintaining it in good working condition?

In this part of the journey, you will come into a conscious relationship with your body and create a vision of how you would like it to be. You will work from the inside out. With a clear vision that represents your truth for your body—not someone else's truth—you will discover how to manifest that vision by creating a body well-being program personally suited to you.

If you have a healthy, fit, and well-cared-for body that you experience as a source of pride, you'll be able to soar to the next level. If you do just enough basic maintenance to get by, treating your body like a utility car, you'll find inspiration to trade up. And if thus far you've only experienced your body as the thing that carries your head around, you'll find the encouragement and hope you'll need to change.

A Dialogue with Your Body

There's no time like the present to get to know your body better. You've learned how important good communication is in having a successful relationship. Now, what about good communication with your body? Have you ever stopped to ask it what it thinks about what you're doing or not doing to it? Your body has a consciousness of its own and would be happy to tell you how it's feeling; all you have to do is ask. When you do ask, be prepared for a lively response. Your body may speak to you with humor, poignancy, sadness, anger, compassion, joy—you name it. Your relationship with your body is a totally personal one, and it evolves over time. Opening the channels of communication will be like making a new friend.

It's time to check in and see what your body has to say. Drawing out your body's wisdom and learning from it is a very special act. We hope you enjoy it.

EXERCISE | BODY DIALOGUE

Allow approximately twenty minutes to do this exercise. You will need your journal. Space has been provided in case your journal is not handy. It is most helpful to do this exercise with the attitude of a compassionate witness, since we often tend to be quite judgmental about our bodies.

The body dialogue has twelve questions. After each question, close your eyes to get more in touch with your body. Once you receive an answer from your body, write it down. Remember to keep your eyes soft and relaxed as you write. Find a quiet place where you will be undisturbed. Sit in a comfortable chair and put on some soft, relaxing music.

Get yourself ready for a chat by taking a few deep breaths to relax. In your own words, tell your body that you would like to have a frank heart-to-heart dialogue and that you want honest feedback about what it's feeling. Ask your body the following questions:

1. How much have I tapped into your overall potential? How do you feel about this?

2. Are you in good condition? How do you feel about this?

3. Is your heart and cardiovascular system healthy? How do you feel about this?

4. How flexible and aligned (the health of the spine) are you? How do you feel about this?

5. How do you like the food I put into you? Be specific.

6. Do you have good stamina and endurance? How do you feel about this?

7. Do you have good muscle tone and strength? How do you feel about this?

8. Do you get the appropriate amount of rest? How do you feel about this?

9. How do you like the thoughts I think about you?

10. Do you feel loved, cared for, and appreciated by me? How do you feel about this?

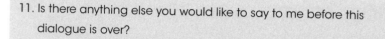

11. Is there anything else you would like to say to me before this dialogue is over?

12. Finally, communicate to your body anything you'd like to tell it.

Generally speaking, people are amazed by what they learn during this exercise, for our bodies are storehouses of information, available for the asking. We hope you received some useful feedback that you can begin to act on and have established a rapport with your body that you can build on. As you get more attuned to your body, you will find that it will tell you when to slow down, eat differently, change your exercise pattern, get more rest, or give it more love and appreciation. It can be a trusted and loyal friend if you choose to cultivate the friendship. As you draw on your body's wisdom, it will tell you what needs to be done to create physical well-being.

A Body Vision

Let's use the body knowledge you have gained to build a vision. If your body could be any way you would like it to be—not society's vision, but *your* vision—what would it look like? What would it feel like? How would it perform? What would it be like to live in an optimally functioning and healthy body?

How you want your body to be is your choice. As you know, our thoughts create our experiences, and perhaps nowhere is this more tangibly evident than in our bodies. Your present body is a direct reflection of the beliefs you hold about it. It reflects your beliefs—right down to chronic aches and pains and excess pounds. It is our thoughts that create the physical reality we experience. If you don't have a positive and clear vision of how you want your body to be, it will "embody" your unconscious beliefs.

EXERCISE | BODY VISIONING

Allow approximately fifteen minutes to do this exercise. You will need your journal at the end of the exercise. If your journal isn't handy, space has been left for you.

Find a quiet place where you will be undisturbed. Sit in a comfortable chair or lie on the floor and put on some energetic music that inspires you to want to move. Our favorite for this exercise is "Chariots of Fire" by Vangelis.

Allow each phrase or section you are visualizing to enter deeply into your body before moving on to the next. Experience this exercise sensually and physically. If your body begins to respond to the beat of the music by pulsating or swaying, go with it—this is a high-energy experience. Allow your body to tell you what to do.

Find your music and get yourself set to go.

1. Allow the energy of the music to pulsate through your body. Feel the beat, feel the pulse. Feel your energy starting to move through your body. Feel your body moving with the energy of the music.

2. Experience your body's energy and vitality. Feel each cell pulsating and dancing with energy. Experience your body humming and singing with vitality. Feel its boundless energy and vitality. See this vitality sparkling all over your body and radiating out from you.

3. Experience your body's strength. Feel your physical strength. Allow yourself to experience your body as if it had all the strength you desire to do anything you desire. Experience your body lifting, climbing, paddling, rowing, or whatever you choose, with all the strength you could possibly need available to you. Experience your body's strength. Feel it. How does it feel? Draw this feeling into your body. Let it go deep into your cells.

4. Experience your body's endurance and stamina. Allow yourself to fully take in and experience your body's capacity to dance as long as you desire—all day long and all night long if you so choose; to run or swim or hike or walk or bike or mountain climb or ski as long as you would like. Feel the capacity of your heart and lungs to pump all the energy you need throughout your body. Feel your endurance. Experience your body's boundless stamina.

5. Experience your body's flexibility. Experience your body's ability to bend and move and stretch and turn with ease. Feel how effortless it is to move your torso, your pelvis, your neck, your spine, your arms, and your legs. Experience yourself easily bending forward, bending backward, stretching to your right, and stretching to your left. Experience that your spine is totally limber, totally healthy, and totally flexible. Feel your body's flexibility.

6. Experience your body's grace. Experience your body flowing easily through space. Experience your body's complete ease of movement. Feel yourself as a dancer, moving through space with total grace and ease, barely touching the ground. Feel your body blowing through space as a breeze, totally fluid, totally graceful. Feel your body's flowing grace.

7. Experience your body's lightness, its buoyancy. Experience yourself floating on a cloud. Feel yourself totally weightless. Experience your

body as completely buoyant in space, a feather floating in the wind. Experience your body as being totally light.

8. Experience your body's muscle tone. See your muscles perfectly toned, perfectly healthy, vibrantly alive. Experience this quality of vibrancy in each muscle of your body. Feel this vitality extending deep into each muscle. Feel your muscles toned to their highest level. Experience this feeling right down to the smallest muscle fiber.

9. Experience the purity of the muscle and bone tissue that comprises your body. Experience how healthy your skin feels and looks. Experience how good it feels to have a body built out of such high-quality substance. Feel your physical purity. Feel this purity in every cell in your body.

10. Experience your body's absolute health. Feel your body as optimally healthy. Experience the sensation and feeling of total and absolute health. Allow this feeling to extend through every cell of your body. Allow it to permeate every organ and every fiber of your being. Allow yourself to experience a fully healthy body.

11. Experience your body's optimal physical well-being. See yourself at the pinnacle of human physical wellness. Experience and radiate your total and optimal health. Feel your complete gracefulness. Sense your purity, buoyancy, and lightness. Be vibrant with strength and endurance. Experience your boundless, unending energy, and vitality. Experience all that is available to you as you drink deeply of the wonder of your body. Breathe this vision into your body. Allow it to penetrate deep, deep, deep into your cells. Allow it to become part of the memory of each cell of your body.

12. Holding on to your vision of this optimal state of well-being, begin seeing your body shaped exactly as you want it to be. Do you want a certain part firmer, more toned? See it toned and firm. Do you want a part of your body to have more definition? See it with definition. Do you want to change the shape of your thighs or buttocks or stomach? See them the way you'd like them to be.

See your body exactly as you want it to look. The greater the clarity and definition of your vision, the easier it will be for this image to manifest. How much does your ideal body weigh? How does it feel? Breathe this image into your body. Allow it to penetrate right into the memory of each cell. Allow it to become one with your core body essence. Breathe it in deeply, fully, totally.

13. Add anything else you need to make your vision complete. What else do you need to achieve optimum physical well-being? Refine your vision by adding whatever else your body needs in order to feel complete. Ask your body if there's anything else you should add to your vision.

14. Begin to experience this body you have created for yourself. In the body you have just envisioned, see yourself moving around the room. How do you move? How does it feel to be in this body? What can it do? Just notice and enjoy it for a while.

15. Now that you've enjoyed this body in your imagination, it's time to embody your vision. Get up from your chair or the floor and step into the body you have visualized. Experience this body as if you were entering it for the very first time, as if this were your first experience of being in a body, as if you were "test driving" it for the first time. How does it feel to be in this body? What can it do? How does it move? How does it bend? What kind of sensations does it experience? Experiment with it as you move. Make big moves. Make little moves. Enjoy its pure physicality. Spend about five minutes in your renewed body. Let it tell you what to do with it. Move it to the music. Delight in it!

16. Bring your movements in your new body to a point of completion. Find your journal and record everything that you experienced. How did it feel? How did this new body move? What could it do? Capture and record your experience of being in your envisioned body. Allow the feeling of it to be present as you are writing. Allow your body to write through you.

Some of the comments people have made after doing this exercise include:

I found this exercise so moving! It encouraged me to claim my new body as my birthright, because it is mine. I feel stronger. I feel lighter.

I've always taken my body very much for granted. I've ignored it. It has done what I wanted it to do. It has placed very few restrictions on me. It has healed when I've damaged it. I really ignored it. This visualization had a liturgical quality to it. It kicked off the realization that my body—all bodies—are God's creation and that means that I have something very special at my disposal.

I feel alive, ecstatic, expanded, graceful, whole, joyous, free, wondrous, liberated, and healthy; better than I've ever felt in my life, aware of my body as never before, in touch with my life energy, my power, passion, and vitality.

This exercise was an opportunity to open up to what's possible for your body, to get in touch with its poetry and music. Through it, you've begun a process of consciously creating your body as you want it. This implies taking responsibility for your body at the most profound level—its creation! This is no small act, and it's extraordinarily empowering. You've stepped into the driver's seat and taken charge. You aren't handing responsibility over to invisible little germs or family history or genetics. Yes, there are certain limits to your reimagining. You can't add six inches to your height, but your overall health and physical condition are totally within your control.

Your body will respond to the vision you hold for it. To make your current vision a reality, you need to feel it deeply in your body, right down to the cellular level. Your thoughts create your whole physical reality. Your body is not exempt from this law.

Shortly after doing this exercise, a workshop participant named Jim went to Jamaica on a vacation. He noticed all the strong, vital, and healthy male bodies. He watched how they walked, how they danced, how healthy they looked, and how strong and limber they were. He realized that he had seen few male bodies in America that were so alive or as inspiring to him. He realized just how impoverished his vision of a healthy male body had been. Jim fortified himself with these rich images.

On his return home, he integrated what he had seen in Jamaica with what he had experienced in the body visioning exercise. Jim's vision for his own body was now very clear in his mind. He began a program to create the body he wanted. He started eating healthy foods, exercising regularly, and feeling good about his body. Each day he renewed his vision. In less than a year he created his body exactly as he had envisioned it. He had worked from the inside out.

The formula is very straightforward: We create a compelling vision of how we want our bodies to be and use that as the impetus to develop a program to create it. Let's look at how to create a program that will allow you to manifest your vision.

A Program for Body Well-Being

This program lays out the six building blocks for creating a healthy, vibrant, and fit body. After familiarizing yourself with each of these areas, we encourage you to follow up with further reading, join a gym, take classes, and, of course, follow your program consistently.

All these elements of body well-being can be attained by just about anyone. If you commit to each of these, your body should serve you well. If you're already doing some or all of these, acknowledge yourself and begin aligning your program with your body vision.

STAMINA

In order to dance, if not all day and all night at least for longer periods, you need stamina. You develop stamina by exercising your heart and lungs, otherwise known as your cardiovascular system. Running, biking, rowing, fast walking, swimming, cross-country skiing, and dancing all build up endurance. There are many resources available to you—people and places from which you can learn about developing stamina. Start, of course, by consulting with your doctor.

CORE STRENGTH

Why do you need strength in your upper body to be in good physical condition? The answer is simple. You use your arms, back, stomach, abdomen, and chest all the time. Also, by developing your upper-body strength you develop a feeling of greater body confidence. You'll know that if you need it, the strength is there.

Some of the ways to develop strength in your arms, chest, and upper back include: exercise machines, free weights, pull-ups, push-ups, and isometrics; for your lower back, stomach, and abdomen: Pilates, yoga, sit-ups, leg raises, exercise machines, and free weights.

FLEXIBILITY

Can you bend your body easily or do you find yourself stiff? Suppleness should be a basic attribute of everyone's body. Yet, unless you do exercises to keep your body flexible, it will stiffen up. Aside from this practical reason for developing flexibility, there is also an aesthetic reason: The suppler your body is, the easier it will be to elevate your movement to the grace of dance.

A good system to develop flexibility and suppleness in your body is yoga.

BODY ALIGNMENT

This element of body well-being is often overlooked, yet we believe it is essential to the proper mechanical functioning of the body. If the structural foundation is not right, everything else gets thrown off.

A car gets out of alignment from bumps in the road and similar shocks to its structure. This causes it to become unstable and begin veering to the right or left. The driver then must compensate by holding the steering wheel tight or turning the wheel a little bit more in the opposite direction. Our bodies, too, get knocked out of alignment through physical jars and ordinary, day-to-day activities. This is compounded by negative emotions and mental stress, which create physical tension that tightens and contracts our connective tissue, causing even more structural imbalance. As the body is forced further and further out of alignment, we unconsciously compensate by putting stress on other muscles and soon grow accustomed to the imbalance.

We can function in this structurally imbalanced state. The question is this: How much better could we function if we were well-aligned? Along with the more well-known chiropractic and osteopathic ways of creating alignment, there are a large number of bodywork systems that have emerged over the last few decades. Explore what's available in your area and choose one that suits your needs.

NUTRITION

The old saying that "You are what you eat" is a truism. Your body is built from the food you ingest. What kind of foods are you putting into it? We have a whole lifetime to live in just one body. We can't throw it away or trade it in when it starts to have problems. Therefore, the food that we create it with is vital to maintaining its present and future well-being.

It's just a matter of time before we must pay the price of using inferior building materials. All the exercise in the world is of limited value if the actual body being exercised is made of junky materials. Food with no nutritional value and loaded with preservatives robs our body of its vitality and life energy. It is possible to keep our bodies functioning on the processed, refined foods available today, but on such a diet there's no way that we can experience the heightened physical well-being that more natural foods bring. Fresh, organic vegetables, fruits, nuts, and whole grains are living foods that add vitality to our bodies. And the more locally grown they are, the fresher they are when you eat them.

Combining a natural and moderate diet with a sound physical regimen of aerobic exercise, core strength training, flexibility exercises, proper body alignment, and a daily dose of good sunshine will give you all the building blocks necessary to maintain an elevated state of physical well-being. You deserve to have a body that exudes vitality and aliveness. It is your birthright to have a body that feels good to be in, looks good, and performs at its optimum level.

There is one final building block, however, that is essential to making all this come together. As you might have guessed, it's your mental attitude.

MENTAL ATTITUDE

When you look at yourself in the mirror, what thoughts come to your mind? Do you say to yourself, "Wow, I sure am beautiful or handsome and healthy." Or do you say to yourself, "I don't like this part; I wish my body was more [so-and-so]; I'm too fat; I'm too [this or that]." Do you affirm your body or do you negate it?

How we think of our bodies goes right back into its cells and begins to manifest. The thoughts we have about our body are constantly re-creating it. The metaphysical corollary to the statement "We are what we eat" is "We are what we think." If you think negative thoughts about your body, it starts becoming duller and loses vitality; if you think positive thoughts about it, it starts becoming radiant and gains vitality. Our thoughts create our reality. Our body, albeit the densest part of our reality, is just one more part of it.

One great time to tell your body how much you love and appreciate it is while drying off after a shower or bath. As you rub the towel over your body, tell it how much you appreciate, love, and value it. It will respond. Another good time to converse with your body is when you look in the mirror first thing in the morning—it's a great way to start off the day. Your body will definitely appreciate the attention, and you will become the beneficiary of a healthy and loved body.

To get your body well-being program in high gear, make up a schedule listing the different elements you're going to work on and the day and time you'll work on them. Your first step might be educating yourself rather than starting a physical program. Begin where you need to begin. Then write down your plan and follow it consistently.

For some, the inspiration of your body vision is enough to get you moving on to the next level. Others may be feeling overwhelmed or immobilized by years of nonexistent or sporadic body care. If you're in the latter category, your first step needs to be transforming those beliefs that are holding you back. Let's take a look at some of the most common limiting beliefs that people face as they start caring for their bodies as well as some turnarounds that address these same issues.

Common Limiting Beliefs and Turnarounds

LIMITING BELIEF: Caring for my body is boring and too much trouble.

TURNAROUND: I create a dynamic, sensual, and outrageously fun body well-being program.

LIMITING BELIEF: I'm too busy doing other things to take care of my body.

TURNAROUND: My body is what allows me to do other things and I'm smart enough to put my priorities in the right order.

LIMITING BELIEF: I don't like my body and I can't change this attitude.

TURNAROUND: I've changed my attitude about other parts of myself, and I choose to change my attitude about my body. Body, I love you!

LIMITING BELIEF: I don't believe that I can make changes in my body—it's too far gone.

TURNAROUND: I approach change one step at a time. My first step is becoming friends with my body.

LIMITING BELIEF: I haven't taken care of my body in years. I feel overwhelmed and don't know where to begin.
TURNAROUND: I build a support system of people who help me begin the process of caring for my body.

LIMITING BELIEF: I hate all forms of exercise and I simply never exercise.
TURNAROUND: I reframe the experience of exercise to that of lyrical movement through which I joyfully take my body.

LIMITING BELIEF: I'm not a body person. I just can't get into taking care of it.
TURNAROUND: I engage my mind, heart, and spirit to create a partnership with my body, and together we explore a new way of being together.

LIMITING BELIEF: Unless I look like a model, I won't be able to love my body.
TURNAROUND: I find my truth, am my own model, and love my unique, one-of-a-kind body.

LIMITING BELIEF: I'm always tired and don't have enough physical energy.
TURNAROUND: I take responsibility to think energizing thoughts. My first thought is this: The infinite energy of the universe flows through me.

LIMITING BELIEF: My body is not healthy, and it never will be.
TURNAROUND: I take responsibility to heal my negative beliefs about the health of my body. I experience my body as radiantly healthy.

LIMITING BELIEF: I'll never achieve my ideal weight.

TURNAROUND: My body becomes what I visualize. I have a clear vision of how I want my body to be and I energize it every day. I am my ideal weight.

LIMITING BELIEF: I don't have enough discipline to follow through on an exercise or weight-reduction program.

TURNAROUND: I work from the inside out. I daily reconnect with my vision, and the discipline naturally and easily follows.

Perhaps one or more of these limiting beliefs helped you better understand a belief you're operating under. If so, the turnaround should, with some personalizing, be able to serve as a foundation for your affirmation. It's now time to put all this information and self-discovery to work.

Creating an Affirmation and Visualization for Your Body's Growing Edge

What is the next step you can take to achieve the body you want? You have created a body vision. What affirmation and visualization will allow that vision to manifest? Perhaps it's an outer step, like taking an aerobics class or going to a nutritional counselor. Perhaps it's an inner step, like changing a major limiting belief. Here are the stories of several people who took our Empowerment Workshop and how they handled their body issues.

Bob's story demonstrates the need for time and patience when working on a major change in life. When Bob attended the Empowerment Workshop he was, by his estimate, a hundred pounds overweight. Though many other parts of his life were working well, he felt overwhelmed and hopeless when it came to his body. He didn't know where to begin.

Though he had lots of resistance to doing the body dialogue and body vision exercises, he stayed with the process and did the best he could. When the time came to create his affirmation, Bob felt as if he should make a statement about losing weight and exercising regularly. He tried out an affirmation, but it had absolutely no feeling of vitality or possibility. He realized that he was way ahead of his true growing edge. When he reread the dialogue with his body, which he had recorded in his journal, he realized that his real growing edge for his body was acknowledging the need for and developing a positive support system and educating himself. He crafted the affirmation as follows: "I have an active support system that facilitates the transformation of my wonderful body." His visualization was a support system that included a doctor, a nutritionist, a therapist, and a bodyworker, all lovingly supporting and educating him.

Over the next year, Bob created his wellness support network. In addition to medical and therapeutic support, he also joined Overeaters Anonymous and an Empowerment support group. His affirmations continued to serve as a foundation for the gradual changes he was making. Each time Bob became aware of his next growing edge, he created another affirmation that represented the growth he wanted to see: "I am aware of what I eat. I celebrate my body and grow with the lessons it teaches me. I celebrate my self-love with my daily schedule, nourishing my body with exercise, meditation, and good food."

About a year and a half later, Bob had lost fifty pounds. He decided to go through the Empowerment Workshop a second time in order to revitalize all his growing edges and especially to take the work he'd been doing on his body to the next level. At this workshop, he created an affirmation and visualization that addressed his next growing edge: "I choose to experience my body's full potential, and I commit to exercising for twenty minutes each day." His visualization was bicycling, flying with the wind, and laughing with friends. He committed to his program, lost the second fifty pounds, and began taking swing and ballroom dancing lessons!

Bob's story is important for several reasons. Any major change we make, be it in our bodies, in our relationships, work, or spirituality, requires us to stick with the process. A quote from Bob's journal indicates the patience he needed to stay with his growth, process: "In all these attempts to change and care for my body, I had successes and setbacks. With each of the affirmations I worked with, I learned something more about taking care of my body. Through it all I was learning to be patient and gentle with myself and to keep a positive attitude toward my body."

His statement could apply to any major change we wish to make in life. It is also important to note how Bob continually updated his affirmations as his growing edges evolved.

Rebecca's story is very different from Bob's. She came to the workshop with a wonderful, loving relationship with her body. Rebecca was running three to four miles (5–6.5 km) every other day and had a body well-being program that integrated the six elements.

During the guided visualization on her body vision, Rebecca had a breakthrough. As she mentally stepped into her new body, she had an image and a distinct physical sensation of running the New York City Marathon. She had a feeling of extending her limits not just physically but emotionally and spiritually as well. She felt the marathon represented a rite of passage into deeper self-esteem. It was a symbol of owning her full power in the world. Developing her potential to run the marathon was a metaphor for developing her overall potential in life.

With great excitement, she shared with other members of the group her insight and commitment to run a marathon. She crafted the following affirmation: "I own my full power as I prepare for and complete my rite of passage—the New York City Marathon." Her visualization was crossing the finish line at Tavern on the Green in Central Park. After the marathon, Rebecca wrote and said, "Not only did I complete the marathon, I completed my rite of passage." She had empowered herself to step more fully into her life. Just recently she fulfilled her lifelong dream of starting her own business.

Now let's look at Edward's story. Edward is one of those people who lives a fast-paced life and doesn't have time to deal with his body. He wasn't in any kind of pain, was just slightly overweight, and had enough energy. His body seemed to get by all right, and he didn't feel it warranted a lot of attention.

During the body dialogue, Edward's body poignantly told him, "I faithfully get you around every day, yet you never thank me or acknowledge me. I feel unvalued and unloved. Please take the time to care for me. I can't keep going without attention!" Edward was quite touched by this and he knew it was true.

During the body visioning exercise, he had an experience of how he would feel if he really took care of his body. In his body vision, he felt strong, vibrant, and lean. He saw himself as being mentally and emotionally clear, more alive and energetic than he had ever been before. He realized how much of his overall aliveness he had missed by not taking care of his body. From this self-discovery, Edward created the following affirmation: "I am totally alive and generously love and care for my body through a program of exercise, nutrition, and relaxation." His visualization was the radiantly healthy body he had envisioned. Within six months, Edward was consciously enjoying living in that body.

The final story we'll share shows the range of what's possible with the affirmation/visualization process. We'll let Laurie tell her story in her own words:

> I was four months' pregnant and had been experiencing severe migraine headaches several times a week for most of that time. I was nervous about attending the workshop, certain I would spend at least some of that time bedded down somewhere with an ice pack on my head. During these four months I had tried acupuncture, vitamin therapy, and chiropractic adjustments—nothing really seemed to help.

The first day of the workshop I came to understand that I had a lot of fear about this pregnancy—mostly I was worried that something might be wrong with my baby and that no matter how well I took care of myself, it would not be enough. Just becoming aware of this was profound for me. I came up with this affirmation: "I trust the way I am taking care of my body at this time, and my baby is healthy and happy." To go along with this, I had a visualization in my mind of a small, round baby in my womb with a kind of sappy smile on his face.

For the rest of the pregnancy I repeated this affirmation to myself and visualized the image at the same time. I did this several times a day. I was headache-free for the rest of the nine months, and my new little son smiled the same sappy smile many times during his infancy.

EXERCISE | BODY AFFIRMATION AND VISUALIZATION

It's now time to create your affirmation and visualization. Go back and review your body dialogue, your body vision, and your limiting beliefs. Synthesize what you have learned and ask yourself, "What is the most important next step in caring for my body? What is my body's growing edge?" Then, from the insight you have generated, create your affirmation and visualization below or in your journal.

Enjoy the gift of your body!

Money

As we've been saying about every other area of life: We create whatever we direct our mental attention toward. But when applied to money, the metaphysics of thought gives us more tangible and quantifiable feedback. Are you mentally focused on abundance and prosperity—or lack and limitation? Do you believe that you will be prosperous—or do you believe you will always have to scrimp to get by? Your present financial situation is a direct reflection of your beliefs about money and your ability to create it. Your present financial reality can be traced back to specific beliefs you hold. We will start our journey by discovering what those beliefs are.

Your Beliefs about Money

We live in a materialistic society and, for better or worse, money is the currency of this society. Because of its strong influence, we must have a clear vision of the role we want money to play in our life. Blindly pursuing it is not the answer, nor is denying its significance the answer.

Each of us needs to look carefully and honestly at the role money plays in our life. We need to sift through the different beliefs that we have developed through the influence of our parents, our peers, our religion, and our society. We need to consider our priorities and determine what type of material lifestyle we desire. While doing this sorting, we need to be particularly attentive to three areas in which we all receive a lot of programming.

ABUNDANCE VERSUS SCARCITY

The two most common negative beliefs about money are that there's not enough of it—the fear of scarcity—and that you're not good enough or capable enough to have or deserve it—the denial of your creative potential. These two beliefs are so prevalent in our society that they have come to be called *poverty consciousness*.

The opposite of poverty consciousness is *prosperity consciousness*—the belief in an abundant universe and your ability to fully partake of it. To have a prosperity consciousness means trusting that there will always be enough money to meet your needs and confidence that you can easily create more when you need it. In the past, when much of the world's prosperity came from personal will applied to the manufacturing and exploiting of limited natural resources, this idea may have been more difficult to accept. Today, much prosperity comes from intellectual capital, which is a combination of intelligence, creativity, and personal will—all of which are unlimited.

More Is Better versus Less Is Better

You can determine how much money is right for you by asking yourself, "What will allow me to be satisfied and to learn the lessons I'm here to learn?" For one person, becoming skillful in manifesting money will most support his or her evolution. For someone with other lessons to learn, money may not be an important part of the curriculum. Each of us has our own classrooms; we have learned not to judge people by how much or how little money they have. The key, as in every other part of life, is that you are the creator of your reality. *No one but you can decide the right amount of money for you.*

Money Is Good versus Money Is Bad

Some people believe that money is unspiritual, so they avoid it. *But money is neither good nor bad—it's neutral.* We consider it a form of energy. It's our own thoughts that imbue this energy with destructive and manipulative power or with healing and transformative power. Money can be used to develop ourselves and to develop our society. For the world to evolve for the better, we need more people who are willing to overcome their distrust of money and begin using this very powerful energy for good.

Most of your beliefs about money are unconscious and unexamined. When you begin to bring them to the surface, they may seem to be existential reality and not changeable. Nevertheless, if you want to change these beliefs, you can. First you must identify them, then you can change them. This next exercise provides you with an opportunity to do this.

Money—Limiting Beliefs and Turnarounds

As we said earlier, a limiting belief is like a weed in the garden. Unless you've cultivated your mental garden, it will have picked up weeds. Let's look at some limiting beliefs about money and ways to turn them around. As you may recall, a turnaround statement is a new, expanded belief that reinterprets the way you view that aspect of reality. The turnaround process is a way of freeing up your thinking to be more creative, allowing you to see things from a wider vantage point. Many of the turnarounds below have come from participants in the Empowerment Workshop.

LIMITING BELIEF: Money is the root of all evil.
TURNAROUND: Money is neutral energy. It is my consciousness that imbues it with its power. I choose to imbue my money with healing and transformative power for me and the world.

LIMITING BELIEF: Money isn't spiritual.
TURNAROUND: Money allows me to manifest my spiritual ideas and visions.

LIMITING BELIEF: Money will corrupt me.
TURNAROUND: I need to have spiritual development to take on the responsibility of having and working with money consciously. I commit to my spiritual development.

LIMITING BELIEF: Managing my money is uncomfortable and time-consuming.

TURNAROUND: Managing my money is the means by which I channel and direct its power and energy consciously. I take responsibility for managing the energy I create.

LIMITING BELIEF: People won't like me if I have money.
TURNAROUND: Everyone has the potential to create prosperity. I am not intimidated by those who haven't claimed their power yet.

LIMITING BELIEF: Let's be honest and realistic: I'm not capable of earning the money I want.
TURNAROUND: I have successfully changed other parts of my life. I will successfully change this part as well.

LIMITING BELIEF: I have to struggle to create money.
TURNAROUND: I allow money to flow effortlessly into my life.

LIMITING BELIEF: There is a limited amount of money in the world, not enough to go around with millions suffering. If I have money, it means others won't.
TURNAROUND: There is as much money as there are ideas to create value in the world. I harness my ideas and create financial abundance as an act of self-love and as an example to others. I use my financial abundance to help myself and to help others.

LIMITING BELIEF: If I make a lot of money, I will become obsessed with it and my life will be out of balance.
TURNAROUND: I balance my material well-being with well-being in all the other parts of my life.

LIMITING BELIEF: I can't trust myself to use money wisely.
TURNAROUND: I define *wise* in my own terms and use my money wisely.

LIMITING BELIEF: I have too easy an access to inherited money and don't feel I deserve it.

TURNAROUND: I accept the gift of abundance in my life and use it for my good and the good of others.

LIMITING BELIEF: My spouse earns the money, and I don't feel I have the right to spend it.
TURNAROUND: I contribute my energy to creating well-being in the other parts of our relationship, and we freely share in the fruits of our mutual creativity.

LIMITING BELIEF: Working to earn money requires me to subjugate the spiritual and creative aspects of my life.
TURNAROUND: I make earning money a creative and spiritual activity.

LIMITING BELIEF: Money will not solve all my problems.
TURNAROUND: I now have one less problem.

EXERCISE | LIMITING BELIEFS ABOUT MONEY

The limiting beliefs and turnarounds above should have warmed you up. Now it is time to go into your mental garden and do some weeding. This limiting-belief exercise is similar to the one you did for sexuality. First you identify your limiting beliefs, then you replace them with turnaround statements.

The primary purpose of this exercise is to mentally clear your limiting beliefs. Don't fret over getting the turnaround worded perfectly. Right now you will remove weeds; later you can focus on planting.

As you bring your beliefs to the surface, you may discover that some are deep-rooted and difficult to turn around. You will probably find some that ultimately have very little to do with money. By all means take advantage of some of the turnarounds listed above. If they don't directly address your issue, spend some time thinking about your most positive vision for this aspect of your relationship with money. If this still doesn't produce a turnaround, be gentle and patient with yourself—it will come in time. The process of collecting these beliefs has taken a whole lifetime; the process of removing them may take a little while.

Some of the most common places to look for weeds in your money garden are in your attitudes about the following issues:

- abundance versus scarcity
- your ability to create prosperity
- religious and spiritual programming
- parents
- your cultural belief system
- male and female programming
- personal spending patterns
- the nature of money itself.

Allow twenty to thirty minutes to do this exercise. You will need your journal. Space has been left in case you don't have it handy.

Write down your limiting beliefs about money. Concentrate only on your limiting beliefs and do not think about their turnarounds. Number them as you go.

When you feel you have written down all the limiting beliefs you can find, begin turning them around. Start with the ones that you consider the most important to turn around. Don't worry if you can't turn them around perfectly; just do the best you can.

Creating a Vision and Plan for Financial Well-Being

Now that you have some clarity about what you believe about money, you're ready for the next step—creating a financial vision and setting up a plan for manifesting it. The questions you need to answer are these: How much money do you want? How much surplus do you need to feel secure? Who can support you in manifesting this vision? What is the next step you must take to manifest your financial vision?

Easy questions, right? As you consider these questions, notice what feelings surface. For some, the thought of creating a financial vision using real numbers is scary. Some common fears include:

- I'm petrified when it comes to dealing with numbers.
- I don't have the ability to increase my income.
- If I go for what I want and don't succeed, I'll be a failure, so I'd better not try.
- I don't know how to make money.

For others, the prospect of taking control of the financial part of their lives is highly exciting and motivating.

During this exercise, notice what you're feeling each moment. What beliefs are being triggered in you? Be attentive to your inner process and use it to further uncover your beliefs about yourself and money. You will learn volumes if you're attentive. If you discover that you have more mental clearing to do, write down your limiting beliefs and create turnaround statements. If questions about work and career come up, hold them for the next chapter. Your purpose for now is to clarify what material well-being looks like to you. When this is clear, you can then develop a strategy for manifesting it.

One way to decide how much money you want is by determining what you want to spend it on in the next year. Your list might include things such as home furnishings, travel, clothes, personal development, children's education, health care, and the ability to contribute to or create activities that are making a better world. You may also want to earn enough money so you can take time to do non–income-producing activities, such as retreats, extended travel, service projects, and artistic creation. Money can represent free time for personal development or social development. This is one of our favorite uses for our money. It's a reverse of the old saying that "Time is money." In this case, money is time.

To determine the dollar amount you want one year from today, you must work from your present sources of income. However, don't be afraid to choose a number that is a little daring and adventurous. As we noted in the manifestation section of this book, the universe operates in unseen and mysterious ways. As soon as we believe in our vision, we find ourselves attracting the worldly "nutrients" we need to manifest it. Money can come to us in ways that we could never imagine or dream up.

Jill was a banker with a fixed salary. She did this exercise and decided to really stretch. She didn't know where the money would come from, but she affirmed that it would come. At the end of the year there was a change in her bank's bonus policy, and bonuses were awarded strictly on merit. Jill was determined to be the most worthy and received 40 percent of the money in the pool. With this extra bonus, she received exactly what she had been affirming.

A similar situation occurred for Alan. He ran a rock and mineral retail store and affirmed and visualized that his sales would double in the next month. He put his full intention and belief behind what he was affirming. Suddenly, expensive crystals that had been lying around his store collecting dust began selling. At the end of the month, he counted up the totals and discovered that his sales had doubled.

Because money is the most quantifiable area of life, the manifestation process is most obvious here. It doesn't work any more powerfully here than in other parts of life; it's just more recognizable. We have many letters from people who attended our workshop, opened up their vision of what they thought was possible for them financially, and manifested what they affirmed. Anyone willing to clear away their limiting beliefs and believe in their financial vision will set the internal and external forces in motion to manifest it. *The key idea here is to clear your limiting beliefs and believe firmly in your vision.* Everything unfolds from this foundation.

Now, fill in the following blank:

One year from now I have a minimum annual income or net worth of $_____.

If you are creating your financial vision for five years from today, the possiblities open up dramatically. If you come up with a new business idea in Chapter 10, "Work," in five years it could be phenomenally successful.

The next question asks you to think about your long-term vision for material well-being. Having a clear vision will help you considerably in deciding how to invest your energy over the next five years. It is important to recognize, however, that committing yourself to creating a lot of money means committing yourself to investing a lot of your energy in income-producing activity. Money returns to you as a result of the investment of your energy. It is a crystallization of your physical, mental, and psychic energy. If you do decide to create financial prosperity, the knowledge you have learned and tools you have will assist you greatly.

I have a minimum income or net worth of $_____ in five years.

Inherent in the idea of investment is surplus. It means you have generated more money then you need for your basic needs. Developing surplus income is like a farmer building a grain bin. The farmer expects a surplus and plans for it. If the farmer does not plan for surplus, he will not harvest beyond his basic needs. It's the same with us: *If we don't have a plan for how we will use money beyond our basic needs, we won't expend our energy beyond that point.* We unconsciously stop the flow of our psychic and mental energy when we reach the limit of our vision. *If our vision is just enough money to get by, that's what we create.* If our vision is one of surplus, then that's what we create. Our thoughts create our reality, a mantra you should know by heart by now.

One of the most graphic examples of this phenomenon of generating just the amount of money you expect and no more is in the field of sales. It is a well-known in the sales industry that salespeople sell just enough to meet the goal they set for themselves. They pace the output of their mental and psychic energy to create the amount of money they expect. The key is expectation.

Once you decide you're going to create surplus, you need to determine a definite amount that you want and a definite place to put it. To come up with this amount, ask yourself, "How much money beyond my basic needs do I require in order to feel secure?" One equation people find helpful is to have at least enough to cover their basic needs for six months in case they get ill. Beyond a minimal surplus, what amount would give you the most security? If you doubt your ability to manifest money, you might need a lot of money to feel secure. If you feel very confident of your moneymaking abilities and have a high degree of trust, you may feel secure with considerably less.

After you have come up with a number that represents how much, then you need to decide where you will invest this money. The most secure investments provide a modest and safe rate of return. If you want to invest more speculatively, make sure that the money you use for this is above and beyond what you need to feel secure. Then carefully educate yourself and seek advice from a competent financial advisor.

It's also important to recognize that your surplus money is your surplus energy. How you invest it is a personal statement about what you want to support with your energy. Today, many people are putting their money in money market funds that invest in socially responsible businesses. These money market funds produce comparable and, in some cases, better yields than ordinary money market funds. Consider carefully what your money is being used for when you're deciding where to invest it.

Now, fill in the following blank:

Three years from today, I will have created a surplus of $_____.

The better your personal growth support system, the more you enhance your capacity to grow. Likewise, the better your prosperity support system, the more you enhance your capacity to grow financially.

To create a prosperity support system, you need to ask yourself this question: Who can enhance my ability to be more prosperous? Some of the kinds of people you should consider including are people you know directly or indirectly who are prosperous, a financial advisor, an accountant, people who can help you work with your beliefs about money, clients and prospective clients, and people in your field who are financially successful. *The primary criterion for selecting these people is that they can support you in becoming prosperous and successful, either by example, by offering advice, or by sending future business your way.*

If you are seeking someone to act as a role model, approach people who could serve this purpose for you. Tell them you'd like to learn what allowed them to become prosperous and successful. In most cases, they will be quite cooperative, honored to be held in such high esteem by you. As you listen to them tell their stories, always keep in mind your own unique truth. You are seeking to cull their wisdom and apply it to your personal style and way of being in the world. You are not attempting to become a copy of them.

My life is filled with people who are helping me become prosperous and successful. Describe both the types and specific people.

You've set your sights on how much money you want to create and who can help you. What is the next step you need to take to translate your vision into action? It may be to seek out a financial advisor to help you explore your financial options. It may be to assess how what you are presently doing can generate more money. Perhaps you can increase the number of your clients, become more entrepreneurial, raise your fees, ask for a raise, or start another business on the side. If your next action is work-related, you will be well-primed for the next chapter.

Take time to consider the next action you will take. Let this action provide the momentum to generate the next action, and so forth. A journey of a thousand miles begins with the first step. Let your first step on the path to abundance be one that begins making your goal real to you.

To manifest my financial vision my next action step is:

Creating an Affirmation and Visualization for Your Money Growing Edge

What is your growing edge for money? Maybe it's to turn around a particularly challenging limiting belief. Perhaps it's to further develop some part of the work you did on your financial vision and plan. To help you determine your growing edge, we'll share some stories of how other people worked on their money growing edge.

Chris was constantly struggling with money; he knew this would be an important part of the empowerment journey for him. As he did the limiting-belief exercise, he was astonished at how many deeply felt limiting beliefs he uncovered. They all seemed to boil down to the idea that there wasn't enough money and so he'd better hold on to what he had. He came to realize that his poverty consciousness had a profound impact on how he lived his life. He kept a job he didn't really like because it was safe and secure; lived in a house he had long outgrown; never took a vacation because he needed to save the money. Chris realized that he was holding back, afraid to live his life fully for fear that there wouldn't be enough money later. With this awareness came sadness and a yearning to change his attitude.

Chris understood that he needed to overcome his fear of scarcity. He crafted this affirmation: "I am abundant and live my life fully trusting in an abundant universe." His visualization was seeing himself in a beautiful house in the country. About a year after Chris created this affirmation and the accompanying visualization, we received the following letter:

Since I last saw you, the most dramatic change in my life has come from changing my beliefs from scarcity to abundance. Over and over I have used my affirmation, "I am abundant and live my life fully trusting in an abundant universe." With this belief as my new friend, I have exceeded the projections in my financial plan and have made the following changes in my life. I resigned from my job of nine years and quickly thereafter received three job offers. One of them was exactly the kind of job I wanted, and it was double my former salary. I sold my home and bought a new home in exactly the place I had always wanted to live. I furnished it just as I had visualized it. Furthermore, between leaving my old job and taking my new one, I took a six-week vacation. Thank you for helping me change my life!

When people open up to living in abundance rather than the fear of lack, dramatic changes are set in motion.

Linda had absolutely no relationship with money. She struggled through the limiting-belief and turnaround exercise and was overwhelmed by the notion of creating a financial vision and plan. In her journal she tells her own story:

> Dealing with money is earth-shattering for me. Having to think about it has touched such a raw nerve. I am intimidated and afraid of it. I have lived my whole life thinking I don't have to deal with money. It is not a reality for me. I have never thought of planning any kind of financial future for myself. It never occurred to me that I could have any control over this part of my life.

Linda decided that before she could create a financial vision, she needed to learn to think positively about money. Her affirmation was this: "I have a positive relationship with money and it empowers me." Her visualization was walking down a pathway lined on both sides by money trees, which increased in size and number the farther along she went. Linda found her growing edge in money and took the appropriate first step.

Larry was someone who just managed to get by financially. He believed that thinking about money eroded his spirit, so he never thought about it and never had any. His insight after doing the limiting belief and turnaround was that desiring material well-being was a healthy, normal part of living in a material world. It was *as* important and not *more* important than caring for the emotional and spiritual parts of his life.

This was a breakthrough for Larry. He became excited as he worked on his financial plan and began to devote positive energy to this ignored part of his life. He crafted this affirmation: "I generously nurture the money part of my life and create a materially and spiritually balanced life." In his visualization he was standing on a mountaintop basking in the radiant sunshine in his best hiking gear.

About a year and a half after he took the Empowerment Workshop, he sent us a letter. He fulfilled the projections of his one-year financial prosperity plan and, as a result, he was experiencing a newfound sense of self-confidence. In his own words, "With this deeper self-confidence I notice my work as a therapist is clearer and more transformative than ever, my relationship is more alive and growing, and we've just bought a dream house I wouldn't have even considered a year ago."

Beth was the mother of five children. Caring for her family was a full-time job, and she felt very good about her role as a mother and wife. However, when it came to money, Beth felt confused and stuck. During the limiting belief and turnaround exercise, she became aware of her belief that it was not okay to spend money on herself because she didn't earn it. Furthermore, she believed she had to ask her husband, , for permission whenever she wanted to spend money on the household and on the children.

As Beth worked on turnarounds for these limiting beliefs, she was struck by the concept of money as green energy. She wrote this in her journal:

If money is green energy, that means Jim generates the green energy in our family. I generate love, caring, support, and a healthy, nourishing home environment for Jim and our family. I generate the white energy in our family. We need both green and white energy in order to have a high-quality life. I know Jim feels he deserves the white energy that I generate, and he uses it freely. Yes! Of course I deserve the green energy he generates, and I can use it freely.

Her affirmation read: "I create an abundance of white energy and Jim creates an abundance of green energy; we share equally in these energies." Her visualization was great shafts of green and white light pouring forth and mingling together.

Beth learned that self-worth can be measured in many ways.

EXERCISE | MONEY AFFIRMATION AND VISUALIZATION

These stories demonstrate the range of issues people work on in this part of life. It's now time for you to address your growing edge and create your affirmation and visualization for money. Go back to your work on limiting beliefs and turnarounds and your plan for financial well-being. Also remind yourself about the action step you wrote down earlier. Take this information and condense it into a succinct statement of the next place of growth in the area of money. Refine this statement to its essence and write your affirmation and visualization in your journal or in the space below.

Work

"When you work you fulfill a part of earth's furthest dream assigned to
you when that dream was born, and in keeping with labour you are in
truth loving life. And to love life through labour is to be intimate with life's
inmost secret. And what is it to work with love? Is it to weave the cloth with
threads drawn from your heart, even as if your beloved were to wear that
cloth, it is to build a house with affection, even as if your beloved were to
dwell in that house. It is to sow seeds with tenderness and reap the harvest
with joy, even as if your beloved were to eat the fruit. It is to charge all
things you fashion with a breath of your own spirit, and to know that all the
blessed dead are standing about you and watching.

"Work is love made visible. And if you cannot work with love but only with
distaste, it is better that you should leave your work and sit at the gate of the
temple and take alms from those who work with joy. For if you bake bread
with indifference, you bake a bitter bread that feeds but half man's hunger.
And if you grudge the crushing of the grapes, your grudge distills a poison
in the wine. And if you sing though as angels, and love not the singing, you
muffle man's ears to the voices of the day and the voices of the night."

—Kahlil Gibran, The Prophet

What allows you to work with love? Love is manifest through work
that is an expression of your innermost calling; work that is worthy of
your highest effort; work that reflects your deepest caring for other
people. It is your absolute right and privilege to experience work as
the blessed gift it is meant to be.

To be truly fulfilled in your life, you must do work that you love,
work that enlivens you and brings forth your passion. To settle for
anything less is to deny yourself one of life's great treasures. And the
truth is that you can create your work the way you want it. With a clear
vision, inspiration, and proper understanding of how to go about it,
you can create your work exactly the way you want it.

People generally view their work in one of five ways. See where
you fit:

FULFILLING

You are already doing work that you experience as love made visible. You have created a work situation that is deeply fulfilling to your mind, heart, spirit, and body. It is challenging you to grow both personally and professionally. You experience deep meaning in how you are using your life. Your work is your play. You are very blessed. Your work vision revolves around how good it can get.

For you, this chapter is an opportunity to push back the limits of what you consider possible in your present work.

UNSATISFYING

You are not doing work that is satisfying. Your work may not be challenging or aligned with your personal values, or give you a sense of meaning. Your working conditions may not be tolerable. Whatever the reason, your present work is not where you want to be.

This chapter will grant you a reprieve from a dissatisfied work life. It will give you an opportunity to envision and learn how to create the kind of work you would like.

JUST GETTING BY

You neither like nor dislike your present work. You go to work each day, and although there's nothing offensive about your work, it doesn't excite you and engage your passion. Perhaps you've fallen into a rut and are bored or burned out. Perhaps you don't face many challenges at work.

Sometimes by making certain subtle but strategic shifts in your thinking, you can fall back in love with your work. You can create a work situation that reengages your passion. In this chapter, we will look with you for those leverage points that can elevate the quality of your work experience.

A STEPPING-STONE

You do work that you know is not your final destination, but is a stepping-stone toward it. Work is providing you with training and experience in a field you will either stay in or which can be adapted to another similar field. You are learning practical skills and your work is basically fulfilling. You still face a learning curve.

You will have an opportunity in this chapter to make sure this step is still relevant, to sharpen your vision of where your path will ultimately lead, and to make sure you are getting the most out of your present situation.

TRANSITION

You are between jobs and wide open to what's next. You may be searching for a new career in a field in which you have no experience or you may want to continue in your current field of work. Perhaps you need time to just be before you get back into work, or perhaps you're actively searching for your next job.

You are in an excellent position to start with a clean slate. You will be able to clarify your vision and make sure your next work experience is all that you want it to be.

Creating Your Ideal Vision for Work

For your work to be love made visible, you need to love your work. The purpose of this next exercise is to create a vision for your work that represents what you would most love to do. Your vision may be a more fulfilling version of what you're already doing or it may be very different from your current work experience.

If you could create the work you wanted, what would it look like? If all your talents, gifts, imagination, creativity, and uniqueness were completely engaged, what would your work look like? If your mind, heart, body, and spirit were totally integrated, and this integration were fully expressed in your work, what would it look like? If your highest personal and social values were represented by your work, what would it look like? If who you are at the deepest level formed the core of your work, what would that work be? If someone gave you permission to do any kind of work on earth, regardless of prior training or experience, what would you choose?

We can have our work be all that we can envision. But first we need a vision. With a clear vision, a firm commitment, and the knowledge to bring it about, we embark on an odyssey to discover our full potential. This potential not only nourishes your soul, it nourishes your body. Michael Phillips, developer of MasterCard and author of *The Seven Laws of Money*, says:

> The hardest thing to convince people of is a fact that only the very rich know. The way to make money is to do exactly what you want to do and do it exactly the way you want to do it. True, you have to make adjustments to marketplace realities as you go along, but the principal way to achieve wealth is to hew as closely as possible to your own inner vision. Only your own idea can fuel you with the energy and passion to continue during the inevitable early discouragements.

During this exercise, give yourself permission to let go of your previous expectations, your past experience, and your past training, and allow your heart and passion to speak to you. The key is not to let the past weigh you down as your vision takes flight. You can pick up your reasonableness, skills, and past experience again at the other end of this visioning exercise. In all likelihood you will build on them.

EXERCISE | YOUR IDEAL WORK VISION

Allow approximately twenty minutes to do this exercise. You will need your journal and colored pens, colored pencils, or drawing materials to draw images. Space has been left in case you don't have your journal. Find a quiet place where you will be undisturbed. Sit in a comfortable chair and put on some quiet, relaxing music.

This guided visualization is divided into nine questions. After each question, close your eyes so you can more easily connect with your imagination and creativity. When you're ready, with soft eyes, record your response in your journal or in this book.

Take several deep breaths and allow yourself to connect with your visionary self. When you're ready, go to the first question.

1. In your highest vision for your work, what does your environment look like? Are you indoors or outdoors? Are you in an office, your home, or somewhere else? What are the aesthetics and feeling of your environment? If you're indoors, what do you see when you look out the window?

2. In your highest vision for work, what must you be doing to make your heart sing? Describe this at the most essential level and then flesh it out in more detail.

3. In your highest vision for your work, what values do you operate by?

4. In your highest vision for your work, what talents, gifts, life experiences and qualities of your being are you expressing so that all of you is fully engaged?

5. In your highest vision for your work, how is it structured? Are you working on your own or with others? Are you managing others? Are you traveling? How many hours a day, or days a week, or weeks a year do you work? Do you own your own business or do you work for someone else?

6. In your highest vision for your work, what challenges do you have that allow you to grow and stretch?

7. In your highest vision, how are you being acknowledged for your effort so that you feel fully valued and appreciated?

8. In your highest vision for your work, describe the effect your presence has on the people you work with.

9. Add anything you need to round out and complete your highest vision of how you would like your work to be.

Take a few moments to immerse yourself in the totality of the vision you have just created. How does it feel to experience your highest vision for your work? Allow this feeling into your body. Let it gently into your heart. Experience this feeling in your mind. Let it permeate your spirit. Allow yourself to fully own and accept your vision as something that is available to you.

After this exercise, people generally feel quite excited. You may have discovered a whole new way to express yourself in your work and life in general. Or you may have confirmed that you're already doing what you love and your only task is to tune up your vision. Some people envision something they can start working on tomorrow; for others it will take some time. Perhaps you need more training or experience, or time to reflect on what you discovered. You can take as much time as you need. You now have a blueprint of what you want to build, and you can move as quickly or as slowly as you desire. You can determine the right pace for you.

A professor who did this exercise in the Empowerment Workshop wrote to us later with his story:

This experience opened up my intuitive sense of the world that has been so constrained in the academic world. My academic success has depended on linear thinking, and I believe I am very good at it. But

I was afraid to guide it with my other dimensions, so I limited my insights, often not connecting with my sensing and intuition.

Bringing the two together had the effect of—well, it feels like the two halves of my brain had been trying to reach each other, and the barriers were finally blown apart.

The effect of this was to enable me to make connections between the many disparate areas of research and thinking that I have immersed myself in for years. I am an integrative thinker and had put many pieces of the puzzle together before. But the sections never joined. After the workshop, they began to fly together as if magnetized—I could suddenly see the big picture. At this point I believe I am in a position to write a significant work on organizational and individual change.

One woman did not find a specific task, but learned what the feeling would be like in her ideal workplace:

I asked myself the question, "Who am I working with in my ideal workplace?" and the answer I got was "My parents." Looking around, I saw all kinds of other people working there, too. But I just got this feeling that went through me that this was my special place, that this was right. It was like electricity.

I don't have a confident answer to the question of what I am going to go out and do, and yet, more and more images are coming to me of what my ideal work could be like. I'm just putting together the pieces, starting with what I know I want. For instance, I have so much love to give, and knowledge of the truth that life is easy and fun, that we can have it all. I know I can turn people on just by who I am in my work. In my ideal work environment I could perceive the state of the people around me. When I would reach out to them, they turned from being really sad to being really happy, I'd like to do that on the subway or on a bus, to see how many people I can make smile.

I'm less worried now about the form. I kept wondering what the form of my work would be, but for now I'm just concentrating on giving who I am.

Making Your Vision Real in the World

When we glimpse our innermost vision of how we want to express ourselves on this planet, we release our life energy. Our passion for living surges, making all that power available to bring this vision into form. Whether you are inspired to move slowly or quickly, seven essential elements will help you take your passion and make it happen. In our experience, the people who are successful in making their love visible in their work demonstrate these seven qualities. If you embody these already or commit yourself to cultivating them, it's just a matter of time before your highest dream for your work becomes a reality.

A Success Plan

It seems quite basic, and it is. The captain of an airplane has a flight plan. The captain of a ship has a navigational plan. A business owner has a business plan. A general has a battle plan. Without a plan, these leaders have nothing to aid them in getting to where they want to go or accomplishing their goals. If you are to be successful in manifesting your vision for work, you need a success plan. You're already halfway there because you have a work vision of what you want to create. Now you need a plan to move your vision forward the next step.

Go back to your answers describing your ideal work vision and decide on an action you can take to move each of the eight parts forward one step. Use the same creativity you used to come up with your vision to begin realizing it.

You don't need to figure out every detail for how you'll get to your final destination, but you do need to start moving toward it. As you keep your vision clearly in your mind, you will begin attracting opportunities. The opportunities may appear as people who can help you, courses you can take, or special projects at work that allow you to prove yourself. Knowing where you're going allows you to respond to these opportunities decisively. Keep this certainty in mind: Your vision is an accomplished fact, and your primary job is to have fun figuring out how you did it.

SELF-CONFIDENCE

People who are successful have confidence in their ability to achieve their goals. They project that confidence and it inspires other people to work with them and trust in their capabilities. Although they may have their moments of doubt, they believe in themselves, their vision, and their ability to accomplish it.

The way we develop self-confidence is by setting goals and accomplishing them. We don't need to set out to do something major. We just need to stick with it until we achieve success. This builds our confidence and allows us to tackle the next challenge.

To develop confidence that you can achieve your work vision, take your next action step in each of the eight areas of your vision. Each time you accomplish a step, acknowledge yourself and let that success give you confidence to walk further down the path.

INCREASE IN THE WELL-BEING OF OTHERS

People who are successful increase the well-being of others. They take the time to lend a hand or offer an encouraging word. The fascinating thing is that as they help others succeed, they find themselves receiving exactly what they put out. What we put out, we get back.

A man we know ran a successful trade publication for the health-food industry. He was asked for information about the industry by a representative of a large New York magazine publishing company that was considering developing a competitive magazine. He told his future competitor how successful the industry was, who his major clients were, and other strategic business information. He also encouraged his competitor to enter the field, telling him how much it would improve the quality of the industry.

Ironically, he scared away his competitor, who decided that anybody who felt that confident and was that generous would be too formidable a competitor. Ultimately, his would-be competitor became a major supporter of his business.

Wishing others success can work in many ways. It is a pure act that springs from the certainty of abundance. It is a statement that there's *enough*—on this planet, in my industry, in my profession. It's a belief that my wishing you success or helping you achieve it does not limit my success—it will actually contribute to it. Who can you help succeed? Embrace opportunities to be helpful. You will feel good and reap practical rewards in ways you can't anticipate.

PERSISTENCE

This is the quality of our humanity that refuses to give up. It is a commitment to continue firmly, steadily, and insistently.

The stories of persistent people who ultimately became successful are legend. Edison's multiple failures before he perfected the lightbulb; the Beatles' many early rejections before they became internationally famous; Abraham Lincoln's loss of almost every election in which he ran, yet still winning the presidency. Those who succeed have a large store of persistence.

We have a friend who is in the fund-raising business. Extracting money from people is a challenging profession. To accomplish his goals, he devised a very unusual technique. He had a sheet of paper with several hundred names and five columns next to each name. A day's work for him was going through his list of names until he reached fifty "no's." He also would keep calling an individual until he got five "no's" from that person. He literally did not take no for an answer. He defined the concept of *no* as a state of resistance, not the end of the process of interacting with the person. He ultimately was so successful that he became president of the company for which he used to do fund-raising.

If you want to succeed, you need to be willing to accept resistance as a natural part of the process. Most of us don't have to deal with the amount of resistance our fund-raiser friend encountered. Nonetheless, to accomplish your vision you will have to deal with and overcome many obstacles. The more pioneering and entrepreneurial your vision, the more resistance you will encounter. If you are willing to stay with it, you will accomplish your vision for work. The secret for dealing with resistance is not to focus on the resistance, but to focus on your vision. You will manifest your vision more quickly—and have fun doing it.

INTUITION

We can never have enough information to make a decision based only on the facts. Cultivating and using your intuition—sometimes called your hunch, your gut, or inner guidance—is very important to your success. You need to trust what you feel and act on it.

People who wait for what they are feeling to be proven before they act become historians. If that's not your calling, you would be wise to develop your intuition as an aid in making decisions. One technique that is helpful in determining how to respond to your intuition is to think about acting on it. Does it expand or contract you? Would taking the action cause you to feel excited and open or fearful and closed? If it expands you, you are opening up to the flow of energy inside yourself and in the universe. If it contracts you, you are closing down to that flow of energy. Either response may be right, depending on the situation. Your intuition might cause you to feel contracted because there is danger ahead or expanded because you have great potential for success ahead. The key is to be attentive to what you're feeling, then act on it.

POSITIVE PRESENTATION

At long last, some acknowledgment of the superficial things in life! Positive presentation is how well your shoes are polished, the kind of clothes you wear, the neatness of your business letter, the way you speak, and the professionalism of your business card and letterhead. In the action arena, we are judged by appearances. How you choose to present yourself is the first thing someone notices about you—and it tells a lot. It says you care about yourself, and what others think about you. It says you pay attention to detail. It says you conduct yourself in a professional manner. It says you're capable of communicating your ideas. Often, all that people initially have to go on in deciding whether to give you their business or their confidence is your external presentation.

Charlie couldn't afford to buy new furniture for the waiting room of his new office. So he filled it with high-quality furniture from his home to give prospective clients the appearance of success. He knew that people wanted to feel secure in knowing that his consulting business was not a fly-by-night operation.

Anne realized that to be promoted to management positions she had to be able to communicate her ideas more clearly. She started taking courses to develop her communication skills.

Look at your vision and consider the points where you interact with others. What can you do to make sure that the presentation of what you do is as positive as can be?

LOVE

To have your work be love made visible, you need to find ways to integrate love—translated as caring and kindness—into your work practices. It won't be there unless you put it there. Everyone wants love and spends a great deal of energy seeking it out. If you incorporate caring and kindness in your work, not only will you feel happier, but others will seek you out, like a bee drawn to honey. An example of this is a woman who attended our workshop who ran her restaurant with love.

Even though her restaurant was located in a poor section of town and her food was mediocre, she had lots of business. The reason was that she made a point of offering a heartfelt blessing to everyone who ate in her restaurant. She offered her customers more than nourishment for the body; she offered them nourishment for the heart and soul. People were willing to overlook the food because her love for each person who walked into her restaurant was so strong. Eventually, she was so successful that she was able to open a restaurant in a better location and hire a top-notch chef. She then made adding love to the menu her exclusive work.

In your business dealings, don't you prefer interacting with a person who is caring and kind over a person who is not? Who do you give a larger tip, the person who serves you with a smile or the person who does not?

Along with the external rewards—more people wanting to take advantage of your product or service—you feel good. You end the day knowing that many people feel better because of you. These people reciprocate love and fill you up even more. Look through your work vision and find all the places where you can add that secret ingredient of love to the menu you offer to the world.

With a clear vision, grounded in concrete knowledge about manifesting it, you're on track. It's now time to create your affirmation and visualization for your growing edge in work.

To find out what your growing edge is, think back to the ideal work vision you created. Were there any parts of your vision that were blank or seemed difficult? That exercise gave you a positive vision of what you want in your ideal work situation. How might one or more of the seven essential qualities help you in manifesting this vision? Is there anything stopping you from getting there?

To assist you in clarifying your growing edge, we list some common limiting beliefs and turnaround statements below. We'll also share with you some stories of how others have worked with their growing edge for work. Use this input to create your affirmation and visualization for your work growing edge.

Creating Your Work Affirmation and Visualization

LIMITING BELIEF: It's not possible for me to do work I really like.
TURNAROUND: Lack of vision and a commitment to it are the only things that can hold me back from doing work that I really enjoy. I create and manifest my work vision.

LIMITING BELIEF: I can never make enough money doing what I really enjoy.
TURNAROUND: The best way to make a lot of money is by doing something I not only enjoy but adore. I create work that expresses my creativity, passion, and full commitment.

LIMITING BELIEF: I love my work, but I'm always getting burned out.
TURNAROUND: I focus the emphasis of the work I do on people's potential, creativity, and growth. Being around this positive energy continuously reinvigorates me.

LIMITING BELIEF: I just don't have what it takes to be really successful in my work.
TURNAROUND: I have a vision and a plan for manifesting it. I'm already ahead of the majority of people I work with. Watch out, world!

LIMITING BELIEF: I can't do meaningful work that also pays well.
TURNAROUND: I use my creativity, ingenuity, and entrepreneurial instincts to create work that is both meaningful and financially rewarding.

LIMITING BELIEF: If I really love my work, I will become preoccupied with it and the rest of my life will suffer.
TURNAROUND: I love my work and the satisfaction it gives me, and I take responsibility for carefully balancing it with the other parts of my life that I also love.

LIMITING BELIEF: I don't know how to ignite passion for work.
TURNAROUND: I use my creativity to turn what excites my passion into my work.

LIMITING BELIEF: Even though I don't like my job very much, it pays me a good salary and I'm afraid I won't be able to do as well somewhere else.
TURNAROUND: I trust in my own creativity and the abundance of the universe to provide me with work that totally fulfills me. I act on this trust.

LIMITING BELIEF: Business is a dog-eat-dog world. I can't satisfy my humanistic needs in this environment.
TURNAROUND: If I believe that business is a dog-eat-dog world, that's what I create it to be. I take responsibility for creating a people-oriented, humane business environment.

LIMITING BELIEF: I can't be loving in a work environment.
TURNAROUND: Business is made up of ordinary human beings who want to give and receive love but who are afraid that it's against the rules. I take responsibility for initiating communication that is kind and caring and create my work environment as I want it to be.

When Kathleen did this exercise, she held a secretarial job that, in her own words, was "pure drudgery." She had accepted the classic limiting belief that work is not to be enjoyed but endured. The idea that you could be in love with your work, that work could be love made visible, was completely new territory for Kathleen, and she was intrigued.

During the work vision exercise, she allowed her imagination to soar and left her office job far behind. Her vision made it very clear that she yearned to be a potter. She had repressed this dream for a long time. Kathleen got goose bumps when she considered the possibility of actually fulfilling this dream! She recognized that her growing edge was to make a gentle transition over time from her current job to being a potter. With this in mind, Kathleen crafted this affirmation: "I take the appropriate first steps to fulfill my dream of becoming a potter and support my learning and apprenticeship phase by income from my present job." In her visualization, Kathleen saw herself selling her pottery at a crafts fair in the country with lots of people buying her pottery and appreciating her talent.

Slightly over a year later, we received a package in the mail from Kathleen with a beautiful, large dish inside and a letter attached. "I have been showing my work at craft shows and people are actually buying my pottery. Who would have ever thought? It's with great pride, joy, and gratitude that I send you this plate and ask you to be joyful with me!"

Gabrielle was quite dissatisfied with her job, and knew she needed to make some changes. We'll let her tell the story.

Work was a major issue for me when I took the Empowerment Workshop. I was in a management job that was frustrating, futile, and assaulted my values and integrity daily. I needed an entirely new career, and I envisioned one for myself during the exercise on ideal work. I created this affirmation and visualization: "The full power of my vision for work manifests within one year." In my visualization, I saw and felt myself in the ideal vision I'd created.

About one and a half years later I was reviewing my work affirmation and visualization and realized that my successful new career was exactly how I had pictured it during the work visioning exercise. I was shocked by how *exactly and completely* I had manifested my vision. Every element—each of the nine steps—I had described in my vision was contained in my new career! I had included in my initial vision flexible hours, travel, the type of groups who would be my clients, the pace and place of work, the teaching, guiding, advising, facilitating, growing components of the training and consulting career that I now enjoy!

Gabrielle knew what she wanted, had the courage to go for it, and created it all.

Susi was a young dynamo. When we met her, she was in a job she knew was a stepping-stone. She clearly realized that her current job as assistant director of communications for a large sports-marketing company could give her the experience to one day start her own sports-marketing public relations company.

But after doing the work vision exercise, she realized that she had stopped growing in her job. She wasn't learning or being challenged. She wasn't getting the training she wanted. She was being lulled into complacency.

Susi decided to take the steps necessary to make her present job more challenging. She created this affirmation: "I increase my level of responsibility so that I have greater challenge and the opportunity to develop new skills." In her visualization she saw herself talking to her boss and proposing a broadened scope of work.

In a subsequent phone conversation with Susi, we learned that she went to her boss and told her what she needed to grow professionally. Her boss' response was to promote Susi to director of communications and redefine her own role, now that Susi would be taking on a lot of the boss' old responsibilities. Susi not only empowered herself to get what she wanted, she also empowered her boss to let go of areas of responsibility she didn't need to hold on to anymore. She also rewarded Susi with an increase in salary commensurate with her increased responsibilities. Susi is charged up again and on her way.

Kevin had a position as an education administrator. He loved his job and felt engaged and challenged by it. When he came to the work part of the empowerment journey, Kevin was sure it would just be a matter of fine-tuning a bit. Little did he know what was around the corner in his growth process!

Kevin had been implementing very innovative projects within the guidance and counseling departments of his school district. His projects were highly effective and well regarded, but in his vision of the highest possibility for his work Kevin found himself changing the role of guidance counselors throughout his entire state.

He visualized boldly empowering guidance counselors throughout the public school system to teach their students the qualities of honesty, reliability, teamwork, and learning how to learn. Further in his vision, he challenged guidance counselors to learn to live what they hoped to teach and to set an example for healthy collaboration between students, teachers, and administrators. His vision included a new, positive curriculum to replace the old, negative one and ways to best implement this. Kevin was startled by the power of his vision. He felt as though he had no choice but to do everything he could to make this vision a reality.

We were thrilled to hear from Kevin several months following the workshop:

> Those of us working with my project have a vision of guidance counselors being very much in a role that empowers students, teachers, and other counselors. We feel it is time to help counselors get out of their offices and away from the tons of paperwork that seem to have become their lot. Two weeks ago we went to our State Board of Education and requested that they budget $250,000 each year for the next five years to enable us to expand the project to include all schools in the state. They agreed, not only unanimously, but more importantly, enthusiastically. The thing that stirs them so is the concept of an empowerment curriculum. Although we call it a "guidance curriculum," we talk about it in empowerment terms.

Kevin decided to let his spirit soar during the ideal work vision and within three months had manifested something he had never dreamed about before he did the visioning exercise. Though he was fully content with his work, he dared to expand his vision and now he's living his dream.

Jack was a senior bank executive who had climbed up the corporate ladder and was now president of a regional bank that was doing quite well financially. He came into the Empowerment Workshop feeling uninspired about his work. He had no new challenges and his deeper values had no place for expression within his present work environment. He was starting to think about early retirement until he did the work vision exercise.

He came out of the work section of the workshop with bolts of energy. He envisioned his bank as a culture that empowered its employees; where they were encouraged to grow and realize more of their potential; where they felt safe fully expressing their concerns; where love, caring, and kindness were acceptable and encouraged in the work environment; where people were motivated to release their creativity; where greater productivity and personal fulfillment flourished as a result. He created this affirmation: "I create an empowered work culture in my bank." In his visualization, he saw the people for whom he was responsible as happy, fulfilled, and productive.

One-and-a-half years later, he had created a task force to develop an organizational culture that supported the bank's employees in realizing their potential. He invited us to do an organizational empowerment training to launch this new program. Jack renewed his vision and aimed as high as possible. He knows that transforming a conservative organizational culture is not easy, but he's thriving on the challenge and reinvigorated in his work.

EXERCISE | WORK AFFIRMATION AND VISUALIZATION

Hearing how other people went for their dreams and manifested them may inspire you to go for yours. Go back and review the ideal work vision exercise and the issues you found that make up your growing edge. Synthesize what you have learned. Then, in your journal or the space below, write down your own affirmation and visualization that addresses your growing edge for work.

Spirituality

What allows you to feel that your life has purpose and meaning? How do you nurture the internal dimension of yourself? Do you have a personal connection with the deeper rhythms of your life and of the Earth? How do you relate to the mystery of life? What offers you inspiration and hope? What allows you to feel deep joy? Do you feel connected to a higher power and intelligence? These questions require us to go deep within ourselves for the answers. Those answers shape and frame our spirituality.

Spirituality is a highly personal and intimate experience of our deeper nature. It should not be confused with religious doctrines. Discovering what allows the deeper parts of yourself to be fulfilled has little to do with other people's ideas about God or with theological prescriptions. Your relationship to your deeper nature determines your spiritual path. Your path is unlike anyone else's path. It is uniquely personal and evolves out of finding, uncovering, and nurturing your inner truth.

People give many answers in response to the question "What does it mean to be spiritual?"

- "To pray, meditate, to love myself and others, and to begin to fulfill what is truly me."
- "Claiming my creatorship and being truth and light."
- "To be trusting and accepting that my inner process is unfolding exactly the way it should."
- "Listening and living the guidance of my inner voice."
- "To be the truth and keep my word."
- "Acknowledging my physical existence as only a part of the universal order; seeking out the intentions of the Cosmic Coordinator."

The purpose of this chapter is to help you create or move further along your personal spiritual path. We will lead you through three explorations that will assist you in this process. The first will be an inner journey to your higher purpose.

Journey to Your Higher Purpose

Each of us comes to this planet to learn and accomplish certain things. Our higher purpose is the deeper reason for our being here. Understanding our higher purpose allows us to have available to our conscious minds those lessons that our evolving soul chose to learn in this life. When we create our lives in alignment with our higher purpose, we have an extraordinary asset to motivate us. Gandhi called it *satyagraha,* or soul force. It is the force of our deeper nature urging us to do whatever is necessary to learn our lessons and grow as spiritual beings. Some examples of a higher purpose might include:

- To raise a family and learn how to love.
- To learn that you are not a victim of circumstances, but rather the creator of your own fate.
- To learn how to manifest a particular gift or talent.
- To trust that there is a benevolent and supporting higher intelligence—call it God or whatever concept works for you—that cares about your well-being and with whom you can have a personal relationship.
- To learn the lessons of caring for people in need of help.
- To learn how to unconditionally love yourself.
- To learn to create financial abundance.
- To help the Earth and our human family through this challenging time in our evolution.
- To learn how to cooperate with others.
- To learn how to play and be joyful.

No one higher purpose is better than any another. To grow spiritually, we each need to move toward fulfilling our unique higher purpose. No one higher purpose is better than any other. The purpose of this next exercise is to help you understand your higher purpose or, if you understand it already, to take it to the next level.

As you ask about your higher purpose, your inner self will communicate to you in an appropriate way. If you don't understand the communication, ask for clarity.

One man who did this exercise was sure that he wasn't spiritual and that the following exercise had confirmed his belief. Frank felt he had "failed" spirituality because he had no meaningful higher purpose. What had come to Frank during the exercise made no sense to him at all. His answer was "a shoe attached to a helicopter!" We suggested to him that he ponder those symbols.

On reflection, he broke into a fit of laughter. His inner self was telling him that his higher purpose was for his soul (sole) to lift off (helicopter). Given Frank's offbeat, somewhat irreverent sense of humor, this image was the perfect way for him to get the message. Frank has subsequently developed an active, relationship with a new friend he calls the Ultimate Big One. He writes poetry to his new friend all the time.

While on your inner journey, keep yourself open to symbols, subtle feelings, any activity that unfolds in the visualization, and, of course, any obvious message you receive. Allow the process to flow easily and naturally in whatever way it does. Our inner guidance is totally available to us—all we need to do is ask.

EXERCISE | YOUR HIGHER PURPOSE

Allow approximately fifteen minutes to do this exercise. You will not need your journal during the exercise, but you will want to have it handy immediately afterward. Space has been left in case you do not have your journal. Find a quiet place where you will be undisturbed. Sit in a comfortable chair and put on some soft, relaxing music. The exercise is divided into several parts. Read a paragraph, then close your eyes and visualize. When you've completed that part, with soft eyes go on to the next paragraph. Get ready for a journey to your higher purpose.

1. Take several deep breaths and allow yourself to relax. Take a few moments to get still and find the quiet center within. In that quiet center, begin to get in touch with the yearning that we all have to understand why we are here, the yearning to understand our higher purpose for being on the Earth. Prepare yourself for a journey in which you will seek spiritual counsel on a very important question: What is my higher purpose and how may I manifest it more fully in my life?

2. Imagine yourself on the outskirts of a very ancient forest. See yourself beginning to walk through this ancient forest. You walk farther and farther through this forest. As you walk, you ponder the question you carry: What is my higher purpose, and how may I manifest it more fully in my life?

3. Soon you reach an opening in the forest and before you is a crystalline, clear pond. As you look into the pond you see an image. You ask this image the question you have been carrying with you: What is my higher purpose and how may I manifest it more fully in my life? Spend as much time as you need contemplating whatever you receive. If the answer is not clear, ask for more clarity.

4. It is now time to leave the pond and go back into the ancient forest. As you walk back through the forest, continue to reflect on what you have learned. You walk farther and farther out of the forest. You walk back over the same trail and finally you're out of

the forest. When you are ready, gently open your eyes and bring yourself back to the here and now.

5. Maintaining soft eyes, write down or draw what you have received as an answer to your question. Describe or draw the particular image you saw in the pond and anything else of note about the journey. If the answer didn't come in words but in some other way, write down or draw what you experienced.

One man, an artist by profession, had the following experience:

The night before this exercise I had dreamed of a blond woman with whom I felt a deep intimacy. She had many other woman friends. Later, I also dreamed of touching my mother gently on the cheek.

I began the journey into the woods very skeptically. On my way, I noticed a peculiar smell in the room, that of a woman's clean-washed, soapy hair, a wonderful freshness. Momentarily ignoring the visualization of being in the woods, I open my eyes and look around to see whose odor I had caught. I am sitting beside a sweaty man and other unlikely candidates; I conclude that I am imagining things, though the odor was so strong.

Back on the trail I approach the pool, expecting absolutely nothing to happen. Suddenly, out of the pool somebody hands me a birthday cake. I am stunned. This is the craziest thing that I ever expected. What the hell am I supposed to do with the cake? I dutifully begin to carry it out of the woods and finally come to rest on a hill. I think, "This must be my birthday!" But why? I am perplexed, but feel light, happy, and [grin] foolish.

After the visualization was over, I told my partner about my unusual experience. Her vision had been of a woman with long blond hair who had told her to love herself. Suddenly, the smell of clean, close hair rushed back to me. Suddenly, the blonde in my last night's dream came to life. Suddenly, I felt my hand on my mother's cheek.

I suddenly understood! My higher purpose is to celebrate my anima's birthday, the birth of my divine goddess! As a result of this higher-purpose exercise I created the following affirmation: "I celebrate the birth of my female divinity."

Another person reported:

As I looked in the pond, I felt a puff of air against my cheek. I looked over and saw this big eagle sitting on my right shoulder. It was looking straight ahead. I realized that I was protected. The next thing I knew, I was flying. I'm soaring over the hills and I feel like a three-year-old. The eagle gave me the experience of trust in the universe. I realized my higher purpose was to develop trust in the universe and that this eagle would help me to do this.

We hope you now have a deeper understanding of your higher purpose and how you may manifest it more fully. If anything is still unclear to you, go back to your pond and ask for more clarity. If you had a particularly positive rapport with the entity or symbol you saw reflected in the pond, it can serve as a representation of your inner self. You can go to the pond and ask this being or symbol for guidance on other matters that are important to you. The more you cultivate and draw upon your inner self, the more adept you will become at receiving inner guidance and connecting with the deeper rhythm of your life.

The Profound in Your Daily Life

A central element in creating a spiritual path is connecting with something that allows us to transcend the everyday, mundane aspects of our lives. This connection allows us to gain perspective and distance from our human drama and allows us to feel a sense of the profound in our life. We need to have a personal sense of oneness with the whole pattern of life that animates the cosmos. We need to experience wonder regularly. An intellectual concept of God is dry and sterile compared to a personal relationship with something transcendent. We can't just read about it or listen to others talk about it. We need to experience it directly.

We can connect with this sense of wonder, oneness, awe, and profundity in many ways. Some experiences that might have transported you to a higher level of consciousness are:

- Being present at a birth.
- Witnessing death.
- A moment of intense beauty.
- A movie or book that poignantly depicts the human condition.
- A lucid dream.
- Euphoria after making love.
- Falling in love.
- An extraordinary piece of music.
- A moment when you were able to laugh at the whole human drama.
- Euphoria that results from physical exercise.
- A profound moment of experiencing nature.

These moments are available to any of us without having to do anything other than be open and sensitive to them. They are experiences that allow us to transcend our everyday reality and recognize that we are part of something much larger than we can explain or understand. The ancients called this *The Mystery*. Each of these profound moments is a spiritual experience that you can use as a point of focus for a regular meditation practice. As you meditate on this moment, your consciousness once again reexperiences a state of transcendence.

EXERCISE | TRANSCENDENCE MEDITATION

Allow approximately ten minutes to do this exercise. You will need your journal. Space has been left in case your journal is not handy. Find a quiet place where you will not be disturbed. Sit in a comfortable chair, put on some soft, relaxing music, and get set.

1. Scan your life and write down those experiences in which you transcended your normal everyday state of mind and connected with the profound in life. Look through the list above for inspiration, but don't be limited by this list. If you had any meditation or prayer experiences that were profound, you can also draw on these.

2. Choose your most profound experience. Take a few deep breaths and immerse yourself in that moment. Experience it as fully and thoroughly as if it were happening right now. Spend at least five minutes being fully present in this experience and allow it to take you where it will. When you feel ready, bring yourself back to your normal state of consciousness.

3. Notice how you're feeling right now. Notice how you're relating to life right now. Notice how regenerated you feel. Use this meditation to spiritually refresh yourself whenever you feel the need. It's an asset you have accumulated in your spiritual bank account.

Discovering Your Spiritual Gifts

We each come into life with certain spiritual gifts to assist us in our growth. Like our higher purpose, knowledge of our spiritual gifts is readily available if we ask for it. These gifts are the spiritual bounty by which we further our evolution and bless the planet. Native American tradition says that when you truly know your spiritual gifts, you are in a position to fulfill your higher purpose.

The next exercise is an opportunity to discover, or deepen your already existing knowledge of, your gifts. It is a very special and magical inner journey.

EXERCISE | SPIRITUAL GIFTS GUIDED VISUALIZATION

Allow thirty to forty minutes for this exercise. You will need your journal and colored pens or drawing materials. Space has been left in case you don't have your journal handy. Find a quiet place where you will not be disturbed. Sit in a comfortable chair and put on some soft, relaxing music. The guided visualization is divided into several parts. After each paragraph, close your eyes so you can more easily visualize. At certain points in the journey you will be guided to draw or record in your journal. Maintain soft eyes as you move in and out of the meditative state. Get yourself ready for a magical journey.

1. Take several deep breaths and feel yourself relaxing. In this journey you will be carrying a question that you will ask of those you meet. The question is this: Can you please tell me one of the spiritual gifts that I have been given to help me on my path? We invite you to take this journey as your child self. Be open to wonder and magic. Take a few moments now to be in touch with your childlike spirit of wonder.

2. See yourself at the outskirts of the same forest you just visited for your higher-purpose journey. As you know by now, this forest is quite magical and has many surprises in it. Again, begin to walk through this ancient forest. As you walk farther into the forest you come upon a large tree trunk with a door. Open the door and notice that there is a spiral ladder leading down into the tree trunk. You begin to climb down the spiral ladder until you are well below the surface of the Earth. You spiral down, down, down.

3. Finally, you reach the end of the spiral ladder and come to another door. You open this door and enter a world of splendor and enlightenment. For several moments you just take in this extraordinary sight, listening to the wondrous sounds and delighting in what you see. As you are marveling, you become aware of your ability to communicate with everything in your environment. You also discover your ability to fly!

4. As you begin to explore this world of splendor and enlightenment, you find yourself attracted to a crystal. You develop a very special friendship with this crystal and ask your crystal friend this question: "Can you please tell me one of the spiritual gifts that I have been given to help me on my path?" When you have received your answer, with soft eyes record or draw what you have received in your journal.

5. Thank your friend the crystal and say good-bye. As you continue to explore this world of splendor and enlightenment, you hear a flower calling your name. Again, you develop a very special friendship with this flower. After a while, you ask your flower friend this question: "Can you please tell me one of the spiritual gifts that I have been given to help me on my path?" When you have received your answer, with soft eyes record or draw what you've received in your journal.

6. Thank your friend the flower and say good-bye. As you continue your adventure, you come upon a great kingdom of animals. You begin to play with the animals. Gradually, you are attracted to a certain animal with which you develop a special friendship. You ask your animal friend, "Can you please tell me one of the spiritual gifts that I have been given to help me on my path?" When you have received your answer, with soft eyes record or draw what you have received in your journal.

7. As before, thank your animal friend and say good-bye. As you're leaving, a butterfly alights upon your shoulder and guides you as you fly together to the top of a mountain. Waiting for you on the mountaintop is a wise and loving person. Again, you develop a very special friendship with this person. You ask this wise and loving friend the question, "Can you please tell me one of the spiritual gifts I have been given to help me on my path?" When you have received your answer, with soft eyes record or draw what you received in your journal.

8. Thank your friend and say good-bye. As you leave your friend on the mountaintop, you take flight, fully experiencing the joy of flying. During your flight, you fly through a giant rainbow. As you come out the other side of the rainbow, you find yourself in the realm of spirit. Greeting you there is a spirit guide. You develop a special friendship with this spirit guide. When you feel ready, you ask your spirit guide friend your question: "Can you please tell me one of the spiritual gifts that I have been given to help me on my path?" When you have received an answer, gently, with soft eyes, record or draw what you received in your journal.

9. Thank your spirit guide and say good-bye. Your spirit guide lets you know it's time to return to your regular world. You begin to fly back over this magical world of splendor and enlightenment, reflecting on the gifts you have received. You fly back over your friend on the mountaintop, over your animal friend, your friend the flower, and finally over your crystal friend.

10. You arrive back at the door that opens to the spiral ladder. You take one more look, savoring this magical world, and then open

the door leading up into the tree trunk. You begin climbing back up the spiral ladder. Up and up the spiral ladder you climb, until you reach the door that leads out of the tree trunk. You open the door and reenter the ancient forest. You begin to retrace your footsteps back through the forest. You come farther and farther out of the forest, until you are on the edge of the forest where you entered. When you are ready, you leave the forest and come back to the here and now.

Spend a little time reflecting on what you have just experienced. There is no rush to move on. Allow the magic of the journey to be with you. When you're ready, you can read further.

The kinds of spiritual gifts people uncover are varied. Sometimes they are intangible gifts, such as wisdom, love, compassion, kindness, integrity, generosity, gentleness, balance, trust, will, sensitivity, leadership, and intelligence. Sometimes they are very tangible gifts, such as organizational know-how, athletic prowess, a Midas touch, healing powers, artistic ability, physical beauty, manual dexterity, and so on. Like every other part of life, there is no gift that is better than another. The special gifts that we each have are there to help us learn what we came here to learn. Our primary responsibility is to use the gifts that we have received to the fullest of our ability.

The beings who reveal to us our gifts are themselves sometimes quite meaningful themselves to many people who do this exercise. If this was so for you, you might find it exciting to reconnect with one or more of them at a future time. They can be special spiritual friends who help you on your life's journey. If you feel the need for spiritual counsel above and beyond what your own inner self can provide, ask your spiritual friends for advice.

Walking Your Spiritual Path

With knowledge of your higher purpose, your special way to connect with the mystery, and your inner gifts, you have all the elements you need to proceed along your unique spiritual path. Only you can determine how to walk this path. How slowly or quickly you travel is your choice. *You are totally in charge of and responsible for your own spiritual evolution.* You can get inspiration from a spiritual group, religion, or teacher, but ultimately the spiritual journey is a solo journey. An interior life that is constantly unfolding and deepening will motivate and excite you to keep walking your spiritual path. Like every other aspect of life, your inner life needs nourishment and cultivation to grow and thrive. Let's look at some ways to do this.

DEVELOP AN ONGOING RELATIONSHIP WITH YOUR INNER SELF

To be in touch with the deeper rhythms of your life, you need to take time each day to relate to your inner self in silence. If the phrase *inner self* doesn't speak to you, choose a word or phrase that does. You can make up your own, like Frank's *Ultimate Big One.* Whatever you call it, you need to take time each day to cultivate this inner relationship to renew yourself spiritually. It is this daily interaction that gives you the energy and inspiration to create a life based on your own inner truth.

Meditation is the method best suited for this, as its explicit purpose is to quiet your mind so that you can become attuned to your deeper nature. Along with deepening your access to your inner self, meditation has many other rewards. Vimala Thalzar, an Eastern meditation teacher, says this of meditation:

> Silence has not been explored in your culture. Meditation offers the silence and balance. In this state of silence there is no tension. The wholeness of silence begins to heal the body and the mind. A new quality of perception, a new quality of response is available to us through the silence. Through the silence we gain an intimate relationship with ourself, the whole, and the timelessness of life.

Whether through a meditation practice or another means for getting silent, a daily interaction with your inner self is an essential ingredient in walking your spiritual path.

ALIGN YOUR ACTIONS WITH YOUR HIGHER PURPOSE

Knowing your higher purpose and the assets you have to help to achieve this purpose is a remarkable blessing. You may not know exactly how to get where you're going at every moment, but you know your purpose for being on Earth. You have a direction. Most people stumble along through life, never quite sure why they're doing what they're doing. They adopt the dominant beliefs of the culture, their parents, and their religion. They never develop their own inner truth and consequently never feel very satisfied or fulfilled.

To stay on your path, you need to continually be aligning your actions with your higher purpose, asking yourself, "Does this activity further my higher purpose?" It's important to remember that your higher purpose has nothing to do with moral prescriptions, or dos and don'ts. It has nothing to do with being religious, yet it can include deep religious observance. Your higher purpose revolves around the lessons your soul wants to learn in this life. When your actions align with your higher purpose, you will feel inwardly satisfied.

DEVELOP A SPIRITUAL SUPPORT SYSTEM

Walking your path is easier when you are around others who are also on a spiritual path. It helps inspire and encourage you to deepen your own spiritual practice. This is the primary reason churches, synagogues, and spiritual brotherhoods and sisterhoods came into existence. A spiritual support group is primarily oriented toward the interior life. While sometimes this can be combined with a personal growth support system, it's important to recognize the distinction.

A personal growth support system is often focused on issues that are externally or psychologically oriented. This complements a spiritual support system, but it is not the same thing. The purpose of a spiritual support system is to meditate together, pray together, chant together, celebrate the joy of being spiritually awake together through singing and dancing, share insights and spiritual experiences with others, and get support and feedback when we feel spiritually stuck.

You may be part of an existing group that, with a little tinkering, will provide you with the kind of spiritual nourishment you need. Or you may have to create your own group. If you do the latter, consider it an opportunity to create the group exactly the way you want it to be. To maintain intimacy and quality communication, the ideal group size is eight to twelve people. Sometimes people set up a small group within the framework of a larger group or class that meets regularly.

SPEND TIME WITH NATURE

Another source of spiritual support comes from being with nature. Activities like taking quiet walks by the water or through the woods, sitting in a garden, and sailing can be very spiritually renewing. For some, this is the primary way of connecting with the deeper rhythm of life. For all of us, it provides an opportunity to slow down and become tranquil. When we're in this state of mind, we can listen more closely to our inner selves and feel more connected with our life-support system, the Earth.

ACCEPT OTHER SPIRITUAL PATHS

As we come to more fully understand that this planet is a school with each of us here to learn different spiritual lessons, our ability to accept others greatly increases. *Our spiritual lessons are not better or worse than anyone else's—they are simply different.* It is to learn these lessons that we create and follow our spiritual path. As we integrate this fundamental truth into our worldview, we feel secure in our own spiritual path and more accepting of other paths. We come to understand that each of us must create his or her own spiritual path. We move from wanting others to be like us, and negatively judging them when they are not, to accepting them. Eventually, we move from accepting others to encouraging them to find their own paths.

BECOME A CONSCIOUS CO-CREATOR

If you were the creator of the universe, how would you like to interact with human beings? Would you like to interact with human beings who couldn't make decisions without asking you for advice at every turn in the road, or would you like to interact with human beings who had developed inner knowledge and wisdom of their own, had learned to trust their inner guidance, and periodically came to you as a friend seeking advice? The former is like a child asking a father or mother what to do. The latter is like the mature adult who relates as one friend to another.

As we travel along our spiritual paths, a maturation process takes place in which we move from a dependent relationship with something outside ourselves to a trust in our own inner knowing. *We move from being an instrument of some higher power to a co-creator with this higher power.* We move from being a victim of circumstances on Earth to being a co-creator of its evolution.

Whether you like it or not, you are a creative force in the universe. You are constantly co-creating the world through what you believe and the actions you take. Taking responsibility to consciously direct your thoughts and actions toward evolving a better world is the next level of empowerment.

The creator of the universe has a role—creating the evolution game and supporting us when we need help. And we have a role—playing the evolution game as a co-creator. When we engage in the game wholeheartedly, our personal evolution and the evolution of the world take place. By expanding the framework of our lives to include helping the Earth evolve, we take our power to a new level. This stretch furthers our spiritual evolution. It's quite a game!

A wonderful story describing this co-creation process is told by Marc Gellman. It is titled "Partners."

> *Before there was anything, there were God, a few angels, and a gigantic, spinning, swirling glob of rocks and water with no place to go.*
> *The angels said to God, "Why don't you clean up this mess?"*
> *So God took all the rocks out of the swirling glob, put them in one place, and said, "I will call this place the universe. Some of the rocks will be planets, some will be stars, and some will be just rocks."*

Then God took all the water from the swirling glob and spread it around the universe, saying, "Some of this water will be oceans, some will be clouds, and some will be just water."
Then the angels asked God, "Is the world finished?"
God answered, "NOPE!"
On some of the rocks God placed growing things—and creeping things—and things that only God knows what they are! And when God had done all this, the angels looked around the universe and said, "Well, it's neater, but is it finished?"
God answered, "NOPE!"
God made a man and a woman from some of the water and dust and said, "Look, I'll give you the whole world, but you have to finish it."
"Now you look!" they said. "We can't finish the world without your help—so maybe—we could be partners."
God warned them, "If we're going to be partners, sometimes you might get angry at me, and sometimes I might get angry at you, but even so, none of us can stop finishing the world— that's the deal." And they all agreed to the deal.
Then the angels asked God, "Is the world finished?"
God smiled and answered, "I don't know. Go ask my partners."

Co-creating the future of our planet with God is the best game in town! No spiritual path should be without it.

Your Spiritual Growing Edge

To find your spiritual growing edge, think about your responses to the three exercises you just completed. Did you notice any limiting beliefs that arose to stop you from making spiritual progress in your life?

To further assist you in defining your growing edge, below is a list of some common limiting beliefs and turnarounds. Then we'll share some stories of how others have worked with their spirituality growing edges.

LIMITING BELIEF: I can't be spiritual and also be financially successful/sexual/powerful/desire worldly things.
TURNAROUND: *Spiritual* does not mean *antimaterial*. I imbue my life with spiritual values, such as joy, peace, harmony, love, beauty, kindness, generosity, and reverence, which add quality to my material existence.

LIMITING BELIEF: To be spiritual, I must follow a code of conduct laid out by a religion/guru/writer of a spiritual book.
TURNAROUND: My spirituality grows out of my own self-knowledge. I trust it and ground my actions in it.

LIMITING BELIEF: To grow spiritually, I must remove myself from the snares of the world.
TURNAROUND: My life in the world is where I practice my spirituality.

LIMITING BELIEF: Spirituality is too removed from daily life to be practical and useful.
TURNAROUND: The more I am in alignment with what gives my life meaning and purpose, the more powerful I am in the world.

LIMITING BELIEF: Spirituality means ceding control of my life to some higher power that's outside of me.
TURNAROUND: God's will is my own highest consciousness in this moment.

LIMITING BELIEF: To be spiritual, I must subdue my ego.
TURNAROUND: My ego is the form that holds my sense of self. I allow my sense of self to grow until it expands beyond the ego container and merges with the infinite freedom of spirit.

LIMITING BELIEF: The nature of life on this planet is suffering.
TURNAROUND: Life on this planet is whatever I make it. My life is about love, joy, harmony, service to others, and oneness.

LIMITING BELIEF: The goal of spirituality is to go to heaven/attain nirvana/become God-realized as soon as possible, and our actions should all be directed toward this end.
TURNAROUND: I learn the lessons of Earth on Earth and nowhere else. My spirituality can certainly include expanding my consciousness.

LIMITING BELIEF: A sign of spiritual evolution is the acquisition of special powers.
TURNAROUND: A sign of my spiritual evolution is wisdom, kindness, and love; special powers are a sideline.

LIMITING BELIEF: To evolve spiritually, I need to master sacred esoteric texts, have a guru, and spend years meditating.
TURNAROUND: To evolve spiritually, I need to learn what I came to Earth to learn. That may or may not include a teacher, scriptures, and meditation.

LIMITING BELIEF: My life is a mess because of my bad karma.
TURNAROUND: I accept where I am at this moment and take responsibility for creating my future. I am in charge of my destiny.

LIMITING BELIEF: The world is full of corrupt, evil people who are leading it down a road of destruction.
TURNAROUND: I take responsibility to create the world as a beautiful and sacred place, filled with beings committed to their own and the planet's evolution.

LIMITING BELIEF: God is a male figure with a lot of power who will punish me if I don't do the right thing.

TURNAROUND: I create God as a loving, kind, playful, wise, powerful friend. We play together, co-creating the universe.

When Michael did the Empowerment Workshop, he was feeling disempowered spiritually. He had recently left a spiritual group that laid out a prescribed path that he was supposed to follow in order to grow spiritually. There were lots of dos and don'ts and dogmas. He had not been encouraged to develop his own relationship to God and his inner self; rather, he was told the spiritual leader knew best and had all the answers. In his recently abandoned spiritual group, Michael didn't trust that he could find his own inner truth and be in charge of his own spiritual development.

When he did the higher-purpose exercise, he broke into tears. For the first time in his life, he felt he could go within himself and get answers to important questions. Michael discovered that his higher purpose was to learn to trust the God within and not to rely on outside sources to tell him how to act and think. This insight was reinforced in the meditation on the profound in daily life. In that meditation, Michael felt a very close relationship with nature and realized that this was an important way for him to connect with God.

Michael's affirmation was this: "I trust my own inner knowing and path to God." His visualization was seeing himself at his favorite spot in nature, feeling totally connected with himself and all of creation.

Joan came to the Empowerment Workshop inspired to work on all the parts of her life—except spirituality. She just didn't know what to make of this part of life, nor did she really pay much attention to it. During the exercises in the spirituality part of the workshop, she didn't expect a lot to happen.

During the higher-purpose exercise, Joan learned that her purpose was to love herself, and through this she would experience the enormous love of the universe. Her growing-edge work in the other parts of life had been precisely about loving herself. She began to feel more excited and intrigued as we moved into the spiritual-gifts exercise. She received the following gifts to help her on her path: a compassionate heart, gentle patience, lighthearted humor, vulnerability, and a sense of adventure. She felt these were appropriate gifts in helping her love herself.

During the meditation on the profound in daily life, she reconnected with a moment when she felt the benevolent love of a higher power in nature. This crystallized in her mind that a loving higher presence cared for her.

By now, she realized that spirituality was not something separate from the rest of her life, but rather an integral part of life that supported and infused all the other parts with meaning. Joan realized that, by nurturing the spiritual part of her life, she was helping all her other growing edges. She created this affirmation: "I nurture my spirituality, and this sprinkles love on all the other areas of my life." Her visualization was taking quiet time to meditate.

Several months later, she wrote us, "I now understand that my spiritual life is the foundation that informs all other areas of life. I continue to be committed to my affirmations and meditation. My spiritual life is growing and sending ripples out through the rest of my life. I am living with more joy and more fullness than I thought possible."

When Brad came to the Empowerment Workshop, his greatest longing was to feel a personal sense of spirituality. He had only experienced spirituality intellectually through books and others' words. His growing edge was to create a personal relationship with something larger than himself.

During the meditation on connecting with the profound in everyday life, Brad went back to his grandmother's death. He reexperienced the mystery of that moment—the feelings of awe, profound love, and the precious fragility of life. He remembered feeling the miraculous largeness of the universe as it enfolded him and his grandmother in both life and death. As he came out of the meditation Brad felt supercharged. He felt that he had received what he had wanted—a personal way to connect with the mystery of life.

He created this affirmation: "I take time each day to touch the mystery of life." His visualization was seeing himself connected to the fragile life on this planet, yet also part of something much larger.

Margaret was a therapist who had been on a spiritual path for many years when we met her at the Empowerment Workshop. Though she was very happy with her spirituality, she was seeking her next stretch in this area. Her growing edge was to find that next stretch and go for it!

During the higher-purpose exercise, Margaret learned that her purpose was to be more than a psychological guide for people—she was to be a spiritual guide. Accepting that she was a spiritual guide was definitely a stretch. She was still considering this new edge as she went into the spiritual-gifts journey. She received the following gifts: unconditional love; light; service to humanity; a still, clear mind; and spiritual vision. Margaret was overwhelmed by the beauty and depth of her gifts.

Margaret became aware that her spiritual growing edge was to fully own her gifts and accept that she was a spiritual guide. She recognized that the primary focus of her life and work with people was spiritual, yet she still viewed herself in a more traditional role as a therapist. The shift she needed to make was subtle, yet dramatic. She crafted this affirmation: "I joyfully own my purpose as a spiritual guide and dedicate my life to spirit." In her visualization she stood with her hands outstretched.

EXERCISE | SPIRITUALITY AFFIRMATION AND VISUALIZATION

It's time for you to create an affirmation and a visualization that address your own growing edge for spirituality. Review the higher-purpose exercise, the transcendence meditation, and the spiritual gifts you have discovered. Look through the limiting beliefs and turnarounds for more insight on your growing edge. Create an affirmation and visualization that addresses your growing edge for spirituality. We wish you fulfillment as you walk your spiritual path.

PART THREE

Returning Home

Always Growing! Making Your Passion Happen

Congratulations! You have just completed a remarkable inner journey. You are returning home with new insight, self-knowledge, and growth. You've journeyed deep into your psyche to get to this point and should feel proud of your accomplishment.

In the course of this inner adventure, you have thoroughly explored your life, discovered what it is that you deeply believe, made changes in outdated beliefs, and crafted new visions of how you want your life to look. In all likelihood, some of these visions have already started to manifest; many more will in the near future. Your growing edges are enlivened and bursting with vitality and potential.

Now you will need to integrate this highly charged potential into your daily life so that it can come to fruition. To do this, a structure for working with your affirmations and visualizations and support system must be put in place. Let's start by looking at how to work with your affirmations and visualizations over time.

Guidelines for Applying Your Affirmations and Visualizations

Nourish Them Daily

The affirmations and visualizations you have created are potent mental seeds that need nourishment in order to grow. *The way you nourish them is through your daily attention.* You can do this in as little as five minutes a day. The key is not quantity of time, but quality of time. You need to be present when you are saying your affirmations and visualizing. Be attentive to any mental weeds or limiting beliefs that crop up in your mental garden. If you notice a limiting belief, use one of your mental clearing tools to remove it. If you find that it is too deeply rooted, back up one step on your growing edge.

The purpose of this time devoted to your affirmations and visualizations is to come to deeply believe that your visions will manifest. It is this deep belief that allows these mental seeds to germinate and come to fruition. The time you spend each day watering these seeds creates and energizes this belief.

FIND A NICHE

To make sure your mental seeds get nourished daily, you need to set up a specific time and place to cultivate them. You are establishing a new habit in your life. To make sure it becomes established, you have to apply your will and plan for it. If you remember that the reason you are taking these five minutes for yourself is to bring the things that are most important to you into your life, you won't have any problem staying motivated. It takes about a month of doing your affirmations and visualizations every day to turn this activity into a habit.

A good time to do your affirmations and visualizations is when you first wake up. You are fresh, and you can energize your day with them. Another good time is just before you go to bed. This allows you to take them into the dream state with you. Another time people find appropriate is while exercising. The state of mental alertness and physical vitality generates high-quality mental energy for them.

You need to choose a time that works best for you and then be consistent in doing it. Commit to one time of day for thirty days and see how it feels. Experiment until you find the right niche. Write down here or in your journal the time you have chosen:

CREATE A PERSONAL FORM

There are many different ways that you can work with your affirmations and visualizations. So find a form that motivates you.

The most common form is to read your affirmation silently from your journal and then visualize your image. Allow it to sink in and impregnate your consciousness. It helps to have your mind reasonably quiet. Taking a few deep breaths will help do this. If you have a meditation practice, do your affirmation and visualization work after you have meditated and are quiet. Stay with the affirmation and visualization until you feel they have sunk in. Sometimes this takes a few seconds, sometimes a minute or more.

Other forms that you might enjoy include:

- Writing out each affirmation one or more times and repeating it as you are writing.
- Recording it with music in the background and a space for you to repeat it.
- Having an inspiring piece of music in the background as you are affirming and visualizing.
- Singing your affirmation.
- Having an artist draw your visualizations.
- Putting your affirmations in strategic locations, such as on the refrigerator, in your checkbook, on your computer screen, by your running shoes.
- Saying self-esteem affirmations in front of a mirror.
- Physically enacting your affirmation or visualization through a special movement or dance.
- Creating your visualization in clay or some other form of sculpture.
- Painting or drawing your visualization each day.
- Programming reminders into your electronic schedule.

There is no one form to use. It is completely up to your creativity and what works best for you. Do choose one form and commit to using it for at least two weeks. This is enough time to see if it's the right form for you. If it's not, choose another one. Experiment some more. Keep tinkering with the form until you find the one that best suits your temperament. You may discover that a variety of forms is appropriate. For now, the key is to become familiar enough with a particular form to know if it's right for you. Write down here or in your journal the next action step you plan to take in creating a form:

How Many to Work with at One Time?

As with the other guidelines, there is no hard-and-fast rule. *How many affirmations and visualizations you choose to work with is a function of the psychic intensity of your growth issues.* If you are going through major changes, you may want to work actively with only two or three and have the others simmering on the back burner. Most people like to at least be paying attention to all the vital parts of their lives, even if they are working dynamically with only their most crucial growing edges. You may also find that you have a very important growth issue that requires more than one affirmation.

Generally speaking, if you don't have any all-consuming growth issues, you should be able to work with seven or eight affirmations and visualizations without a strain.

Regular Upkeep

Because you are creating affirmations and visualizations that are addressing your growing edges, you will inevitably outgrow them.

This is not only to be expected, but desired. It's a statement that says you are growing and your affirmations are working.

How do we know when we have outgrown our current affirmations and visualizations? The most obvious way is when we look around and notice that we have accomplished whatever it is we are affirming and visualizing. This is easily discerned if we are dealing with physically demonstrable issues, such as money, work, or our bodies. However, psychological, emotional, and spiritual changes we are attempting to bring about are more subtle.

In this domain, boredom is an excellent way to identify that change has taken place. If saying your affirmation starts to feel like tedious drudgery, something has changed. To respond to this change, you may need to adjust a word or phrase in your affirmation, change your visualization, or approach the growth issue from another angle. The essential thing is to be attentive to your internal response and make changes in the affirmation, visualization, or growth issue accordingly.

Sometimes when we have been working on an issue and have achieved what we desired, we continue to hold on simply because we have grown accustomed to having the issue in our life. To minimize this, try setting time aside twice a year to do a major overhaul of your growing edges. We find spring and fall to be good times to do this. Without looking at your present affirmations and visualizations, ask yourself, "What are my next growing edges?" They may come out being the same, but often you will find that you have grown beyond those edges and it's time to move on. If this is the case, celebrate the harvest and plant new seeds.

ATTENTIVENESS TO YOUR THOUGHTS DURING THE DAY

A daily practice of working with your affirmations and visualizations energizes your visions on a regular basis. Along with this more formal time, *it's important to be aware of your thoughts throughout the day.* Are you thinking about your visions as if they're successful? Are you seeing images of your visions as fully manifested? When you talk to others about your visions, do you describe them in positive terms? How you think and talk during the day is very significant. It either reinforces or negates the more formal work you are doing.

You don't need to burden yourself by affirming or visualizing all day, but you do need to be attentive to your thoughts. If you find yourself with a limiting belief, simply notice it and substitute your affirmation for it. If a fear comes up, notice it and turn it around. If you are thinking about your vision in the future tense, bring it into the present tense.

Moment by moment, we create our reality. You are now endowed with self-awareness and have the ability to step out of a thought and change it. You have done the hard work of acquiring the self-awareness to *notice* what you are thinking. *Changing the thought* is the easy work. It is a reward for the in-depth self-discovery you have done up to this point.

Designing a Personal Growth Support System

It's now time to design an ongoing structure to support you in taking all the personal growth work you have done so far and establishing it firmly in your life.

The daily stresses of life tend to wear us down if we don't have anything to buoy us up again. In spite of our best efforts to maintain our growth, that vital spark that keeps us on our growing edges often flickers. To keep our spark glowing, we need regular inspiration and renewal. The purpose of a personal growth support system is to provide the ongoing inspiration and renewal to enable you to sustain your growth over time. It may include some or all of the following components:

SUPPORT TEAM

These are people who support you in some clearly defined way. This team might include a life coach to help you focus on the important visions and goals you have now set for your life, a financial advisor to help you achieve your financial goals, a mentor to help you advance in your career, a bodyworker to help deal with physical stress, a trainer to help you strengthen your body, and a spiritual counselor with whom you can share your spiritual life.

These relationships don't just happen. They require you to recognize their importance and add these people to your life. They are your quality-of-life support system.

1. Take some time now and decide who should make up your support team. First, write down the categories of people. If you know particular people who can fill these roles, write their names next to each category. If you have done some of this work in other chapters, refer back to that part of your journal and place their names here.

2. Once you have listed the categories and the people, write down your next action step for each category. For example, let's say you want to begin working with a financial advisor. The action step might be "Next week I start asking friends if they know of any financial advisors they trust." Make your action steps as specific and concrete as possible.

Peer Support Group

A peer support group is dedicated to growth around a particular issue or to growth in general. Issue support groups might focus on relationships, professional development, spiritual development, and so on. More general support groups are dedicated to any of the growth issues you are working on in your life. One of the more common forms is as a women's or men's support group.

After Empowerment Workshops, support groups are often formed by those participants who would like to use the empowerment method to keep their growing edges alive. If you know other people who have read this book, you might want to form such a group. This can also be done with one other person as a buddy support system. A good format is to meet monthly, share your most important growing edges with one another, and ask for support.

What kind of peer support group would you like to create for yourself? A couples group, a men's group, a women's group, an empowerment support group? Research to see if there is an existing group you might join. More often than not, you will have to start your own group. Your next action step might then be to call or e-mail the people you know who would like to be part of a personal growth support group and ask them if they're interested. Write down the next action step you will take to bring this about.

Putting It All Together

Choose a Home for Your Affirmations and Visualizations

At this point, your affirmations and visualizations are scattered throughout this book or your journal. To facilitate working with them on a daily basis, go back through your journal or this book and put them all in one place. The last few pages of your journal may work well for this. If you don't have a journal handy, we have left space below.

When you have placed all these mental seeds in one location, take a few moments to review the work you have done. Celebrate your accomplishment. Acknowledge yourself for the commitment you have made to your growth and well-being. Acknowledge yourself for taking time to examine your life and for how you want to create it. Recognize this moment for the significance of what it represents— you, as an empowered person, forging your own destiny! In the space below gather all the mental seeds (leave the Personal Power space blank for now).

Affirmations and Visualizations   Personal Power

1.

2.

3.

4.

5.

6.

7.

8.

Use Your Personal Power to Sustain Your Growth

It's time to draw on the sources of personal power that you cultivated in Chapter 3—those that provide you with the ability to sustain your growth over time. The seven sources of personal power are:

- Commitment
- Discipline
- Support system
- Inner guidance
- Lightness
- Love
- Finding your own truth

Go back over the affirmations and visualizations you have just listed. Next to each one, write down which sources of personal power will help you to manifest it. For example, you might decide that for your body vision to manifest, you need discipline and commitment; for your relationship vision, you need love; for work, finding your own truth; and for money, you need lightness. When you have done this, you will have a sense of what sources of personal power you need to cultivate further.

You may discover that a pattern emerges, that the same sources of personal power are needed for all or most of your affirmations. This is a very important indicator. It tells you how necessary it is to bring that source of personal power into your life.

To create a fulfilling life, you need personal power. You create personal power in the same way you create anything else—by focusing your mental attention on it. Take time each day to cultivate the particular sources of personal power you need to sustain your growth.

Now go back to the rooms in your guided visualization at the end of Chapter 3 and spruce up or redesign those that represent the sources of power you want to cultivate. If a particular room needs to be redesigned, take the time now to make the room exactly the way you want it. Make the room as enjoyable as possible. Then write out or draw this visualization next to the space that contains your affirmations and visualizations. Each day, start your affirmation and visualization work by visiting the personal power rooms you are cultivating. This will establish the right atmosphere for manifesting your visions.

You have journeyed long and learned much. As you apply what you've learned over the next few months and years, be aware that the journey is the destination. We experience the momentary satisfaction of manifesting what we have envisioned and celebrate the wonder of it. And then we ask ourselves, "What's next?" and the journey continues. That is the essence of life's adventure—enjoy it!

Epilogue

In closing, we want to share with you something very special from our lives. It's the story of how our personal empowerment came to include creating and manifesting a very large vision, a vision of hope and possibility for our world, a vision of our power and our capacity to create the world that we want.

From September 16 through December 11, 1986, twenty-five million people and forty-five heads of state in sixty-two countries participated in passing a torch of peace around the world, encircling it with light. The torch, in turn, shed light on what was working in the world—local self-help projects that were creating solutions to community challenges. This event was called the First Earth Run and it was a celebration of our possibility to live in harmony with each other and our Earth. We organized it under the banner of the United Nations International Year of Peace; our global partner and sponsor was the United Nations Children's Fund (UNICEF).

More than a billion people were made aware of the event through the media. In the United States, ABC's *Good Morning America* provided unprecedented television coverage, tracking the event every week for the twelve weeks of its global journey.

This all grew out of a vision and the knowledge that we can create any vision we believe in—the essence of personal empowerment. As we kept experiencing the empowerment process in our own life, and seeing others experience its power in their lives, it was only a matter of time before we were ready to own a larger vision, a vision of making a difference in the world—the whole world. It was quite an adventure! We'll share some of this adventure and our learning with you from our different points of view.

For me, David, the creation and manifestion of the First Earth Run was a ten-year adventure. In 1976 I organized the U.S. Bicentennial Torch Relay as a way to rekindle the deeper values on which America was founded at a time when our country had sunk into a post–Vietnam

War malaise. The flame was transported through all fifty states, witnessed by hundreds of thousands of Americans, and honored by President Gerald Ford as one of the major contributions to the Bicentennial celebration.

As the flame was being extinguished on August 16 after its journey through America, I had a strong impulse to see this fire continue around the world. That was the birth of the vision—passing the fire person to person around the world to celebrate our potential to live in harmony with each other and the Earth. It was a vision of hope and possibility.

I attempted to create this event in 1979, but I couldn't raise the money or convince people that it could be done. I was not skilled enough, and the timing didn't seem to be right for a global event of this magnitude. Then, out of the blue I was invited to organize the 1980 Winter Olympic Torch Relay that went from Olympia, Greece, to Lake Placid, New York.

My favorite part of this experience was picking up the flame in Greece. We flew on Air Force One to Athens, where we took another plane and then a bus to the little town of Olympia. Just as I arrived, I saw the flame being processed in the ancient ritual form by twelve Greek priestesses. They moved with such an appreciation for the fire they were carrying and treated it with the respect due one of the few sacred symbols on our planet. When the flame entered Air Force One, one of the flight attendants said that this was the most special passenger she had ever had on the plane.

Instead of taking the fire around the world, a billion people watched the fire come into Lake Placid to start the Winter Games. About six months later, I met Gail, we fell in love, and decided to create the Empowerment Workshop.

As we conducted the Empowerment Workshop each month, we experienced a deep integration into our beings of all that we were teaching and especially the willingness to dream big. In 1983, I would get a chance to put all this into practice. The imminent threat of nuclear war between the Soviet Union and the United States was foremost on everyone's mind. The political apparatus was frozen with the threat of war escalating by the month. If ever there was a need for something that could help change the belief system of mutually assured destruction, this was the time. Perhaps the First Earth Run could serve as such a catalyst—a global unifying experience that reminded us of what we had in common, rather than what separated us.

I asked Gail for her help. I told her that our lives—and the financial comfort we had achieved—would be totally disrupted. Gail said, "Is there a choice? If we can make a difference, we need to go for it." And so we did!

For the next three years, we developed the First Earth Run as full-time volunteers, offering the Empowerment Workshop on weekends. I learned what it meant to persevere, to continually refine your vision when you get feedback that it's not working. I learned about all the qualities of personal power and how important they are to manifesting a vision. I learned anew that when you are creating your own truth, commitment and discipline help move you forward, and inner guidance, love, and lightness keep you on track.

I learned how important trust in the universe is when you know the final destination, but you don't know how you'll get there. I learned how important believing in myself and my vision was if I was to get others—from a volunteer to a head of state—to join in. I learned how important a positive attitude and flowing with change were, as up to one month before the event we had not secured our financing.

In effect, I spent three years intensively learning all the lessons in this book and then testing them out on a global scale. They allowed me to be effective and the event to manifest—ten years later—almost exactly as I had envisioned it in August 1976. On that day, my vision was seeing the flame in the General Assembly Hall of the United Nations being passed to the secretary-general by a child, who reminded us why we needed to create a better future. I then saw the secretary-general, deeply inspired, passing it from leader to leader. And that's the way it happened, not all at once, but over eighty-six days.

UN Secretary-General Javier Perez de Cuellar was moved to tears as he received the flame from a child and launched it on its journey around the world. It passed through the hands of millions of people, including most of the world's major leaders, and eventually was handed back to the secretary-general in the General Assembly Hall as the guest of honor in a special session called to celebrate its return. My greatest dream had manifested with all the elements I had envisioned—and much more.

Now I have more than hope; I know for certain that we, the people living on this planet, have the ability to create the world the way we all, in our hearts, want it to be. At this very moment, we have the ability to create a peaceful planet, dedicated to caring for all its inhabitants and our fragile life-support system. We have the ability to create a planet full of kindness, caring, love, and generosity, a planet where people are developing their full human potential, a planet where we can use our creativity to make it a better and healthier place to live, for all of us and for the children who inherit it when we leave.

This is the vision that the rest of my life is dedicated to manifesting. The more who help, adding their variations on the theme, the sooner we can create it.

For me, Gail, the seeds of my future involvement in the First Earth Run were born when I was very young. My love affair with the natural world is one of the strongest memories of my childhood. I vividly recall endless days spent exploring brooks and fields and climbing every tree within my childhood territory. I remember my mother peeling off my wet, muddy clothes and examining the treasures I had brought home from my quests—rocks, sticks, and wildflowers. I was, quite literally, in love with this Earth, and this love of the Earth inspired and sustained me during the most exciting and challenging experience of my life—the First Earth Run.

Another experience that prepared me for the Earth Run was the time spent living and working in other cultures. I saw the bigger picture, recognized how fortunate I was, and wanted to make a contribution toward creating a better world.

Another major influence came at home in the United States. I was deeply involved in both the antiwar activism of the sixties and the women's movement of the seventies. Through both these grassroots experiences, I learned something very important: I make a difference.

The final influence on me was the Empowerment Workshop. Here I had the privilege of being with many people committed to both their own well-being and the planet's. Their commitment gave me an enormous sense of hope that we had the power to make it as a human family.

On New Year's Day 1983, David and I went to see the film *Gandhi*. It had just been released, and we stood in a long line in Manhattan for hours to get tickets. Nearly half the audience was Indian and all around me Hindi was being spoken. Though I had read Gandhi's writings and long considered him a mentor, I was not prepared for the power of the experience that was about to unfold.

I cried through the entire film. I felt as if all the major threads of my personal empowerment were being woven together in front of my eyes: my love of the Earth, my yearning to make a contribution to a better world, my understanding that I could make a difference, and my feeling of hope. The inspiration of Gandhi's life, exquisitely portrayed through Richard Attenborough's film, integrated the separate strands of my process into a whole. It took me several weeks after the film to understand this, but what I did immediately know was that something inside me had shifted. I felt moved and empowered. I wanted to act.

I created an affirmation to attract a vehicle for expressing this newfound inspiration and yearning to make a larger contribution. Within several months, the idea of doing the First Earth Run came back to David, and together we were ready to take it on.

For the next three years, David and I had to use every empowerment tool we had ever learned or taught! My belief in myself was constantly stretched to the limits, as the magnitude of the vision often overwhelmed me. I just kept finding my next growing edge and working to affirm and visualize that I was capable enough to do this. The concept of trusting the universe jumped to a higher level of meaning for me during the Earth Run. I came to call this *radical trust*. Radical trust meant that although I was putting my time, money, love, and personal reputation on the line, there was no guarantee that the event would work. All I had to sustain me was my trust.

Ultimately, the First Earth Run was an opportunity to experience how much I had learned about personal growth and my ability to manifest. I used this knowledge in the most difficult and complex situations. I saw its power time and time again. Let me share with you some of my most precious experiences, which made it all worth it:

In Burkina Faso, West Africa, one of the poorest countries on our planet, a crowd of 100,000 had come from hundreds of small villages to welcome the flame in the town of Bobo-Dioulasso. In an evening ceremony, this enormous sea of African faces was illuminated by candles, which symbolized their hope for a peaceful world.

In China, where the torch was welcomed by President Li Xianan, a million people gathered in Shanghai. We were welcomed into the Children's Palace by laughing children. We were enchanted. They led us into the outdoor courtyard where they taught us songs, dances, and games. I played patty-cake with a young Chinese girl who wore her hair in pigtails tied in enormous pink bows. In this moment I profoundly felt the precious joy of children and our responsibility to their future.

In Nicaragua, Daniel Ortega's child and the child of one of the Contra leaders walked together, holding the torch while their fathers accompanied them. A cease-fire had been declared to allow for safe passage of the torch. What an unforgettable moment of hope!

In the Netherlands, the torch journeyed to the Peace Palace at The Hague. The flame was accepted by World Court President Nagendra Singh and an eternal flame was lit by Prince Klaus. This ceremony was filled with an elegant dignity as we stood in a place consecrated to world peace, with people whose lives were dedicated to international justice and cooperation.

In the Soviet Union, where there was a strong message of support from Mikhail Gorbachev, 100,000 people had gathered in Leningrad to welcome the flame. As we journeyed through the snowy streets, hundreds of Soviets reached out to grasp our hands and touch the torch in a powerful demonstration of friendship.

In Indonesia, eight million people welcomed the torch during its five-day overland relay from Java to Bali. The flame, called the *Obor*, or friendship torch, was received with extraordinary joy and celebration as we witnessed the unforgettable music, dance, and spirit of the Indonesian people.

In India, we were met by President Giani Zail Singh and were greeted with great enthusiasm in all cities to which we took the flame. In New Delhi we merged the flame of peace with Gandhi's eternal flame, placing a garland of marigolds on the sacred spot that honors him. In this poignant moment, I completed the circle that had begun on that cold New Year's Day in 1983.

On First Avenue in New York City, it began to snow as the torch returned home from its eighty-six-day odyssey. As we entered the lobby of the General Assembly Building, I was flooded with emotion as images of hope, responsibility, joy, and possibility from all around the world came racing through my consciousness. I knew that this journey had changed me forever, and I was awed by my love of this fragile, spinning ball called Earth.

What I learned from the Earth Run is that the challenges facing our world today are unsurpassed in complexity. I also know that we have tremendous untapped potential and creativity. I embrace this paradox, and I choose to act with hope as I wake up each morning.

In closing, we wish you much success in creating the life that you want. We also wish you much success in creating the kind of world you want to live in. Dream boldly—you have everything you need within you to achieve your highest visions. We bid you farewell and blessings on your journey.

Acknowledgments

We would like to express our gratitude to the Empowerment Workshop graduates all over the world whose commitment to personal growth have added their depth and compassion to the teachings of this book. We especially acknowledge those graduates whose personal stories are used in the book.

Special thanks are due to those friends who patiently reviewed the manuscript: Ned Leavitt, Elizabeth Rose Campbell, Diane Davis, and Kathryn Hendren. Their careful reading and caring are deeply appreciated.

Finally, we offer our heartfelt thanks to those who contributed to the creation of this book: Anne Marie O'Farrell, our agent, for her indomitable spirit; Dawson Church and Jody Rein of Dell, for their invaluable editorial efforts to bring the first edition of this book into the world; and Kate Zimmerman of Sterling, for her patient stewarding of this second edition into print. And, lastly, Marcus Leaver, publisher of Sterling, who discovered this book twenty years after its initial publication. It is rare for a book to be given a second life like this all these years later. We are grateful to Marcus for his belief in our message.

Afterword

In 1981, we created the Empowerment Workshop to explore this question: How do you empower people to grow and realize their full potential? We wanted to shift the focus of personal development from healing the past and fixing problems to focusing on what we want for our lives, our communities, and our organizations—and how to achieve it. Enabling people to envision their dreams and bring them to fruition was the heart of the approach we called empowerment. The term *empowerment* was new in the vernacular of transformation, as was our approach.

Over the years, what evolved was an extraordinary learning community that became a global empowerment laboratory. We wrote the first edition of this book to share this research. The writing process brought further refinement to our model, and the book's success as a best seller attracted even more people to our trainings. Along the way, we became master practitioners of personal growth facilitation.

We continued to evolve our empowerment work by adapting the model and methodology to other initiatives. Included among these was the First Earth Run (see the Epilogue.) Its success was further confirmation of the efficacy of our empowerment tools.

Building on this growing body of knowledge and experience in large-system transformation, I (David) applied my empowerment expertise to large organizations and cities wishing to create behavior change. The versatility of the empowerment tools enabled me to address issues ranging from talent development, culture change, and corporate social engagement, to low-carbon lifestyles, livable neighborhoods, and sustainable communities. Based on this research I have written many books on these subjects, including my most recent, *Social Change 2.0: A Blueprint for Reinventing Our World.*

I (Gail) applied the empowerment methodology to developing an advanced training program that integrated spiritual growth with social and ecological responsibility. This training became a model for engaged spirituality, balancing inner development with outer service. Based on this work, I wrote *The Rhythm of Compassion: Caring for Self, Connecting with Society*, and *Circle of Compassion*, a book of meditations. My most recent book *Returning to My Mother's House: Taking Back the Wisdom of the Feminine*, explores women's empowerment.

The results from our research, writing, and practice—a robust and rigorously tested transformational model—have stood the test of time. While we were now recognized worldwide as leading authorities on empowerment and our work had gained widespread recognition, we realized there was a next level. It was to create an in-depth program for the mastery of empowerment and transformative social change. To accomplish this, in 2001 we created the Empowerment Institute Certification Program. Since then, our institute has attracted a remarkable group of cutting-edge change agents and social entrepreneurs from all over the planet, dedicated to empowering people and transforming our world—one person, community, and organization at a time. The empowerment impulse we had spent the last three decades bringing into the world had now matured into its full potential.

To learn about the Empowerment Institute or our other training programs, visit www.empowermenttraining.com. To learn about the application of empowerment to organizational and societal change, visit www.empowermentinstitute.net and www.socialchange2.com.

Index

Abundance, 13, 147–148, 150, 152, 159, 160–161, 162, 187.

Affirmations
attention for, 212–213, 216–217
on change, 69–70
collecting, 220
commitment to, 42
on core beliefs, 70–74, 83–84
definition of, 24
on emotions, 83–84, 87
forms of, 213–214
manifestation using, 24–29
meditation and, 214
mental clearing in, 106
on money, 159–163
nourishing, 33
number of, 215
passion in, 26
personal, 27–28
on physical body, 142–146
positive, 24–25
on positive attitude, 69, 72–74
on relationships, 96, 99–101, 105, 107
sabotaging, 28
on self-esteem, 68, 71–72
on self-responsibility, 68
on sexuality, 122–124
specific, 25–26
on spirituality, 209
succinct, 25
on trust in universe, 68–69
updating, 215–216
on work, 179–184, 185
writing, 24

Attraction, law of, 33
Awareness, 3, 10, 11. *See also* Self-awareness

B

"Being in the flow," 37–38
Being, state of, 6–7
Beliefs
affirmations on, 70–74, 83–84
change and, 62, 66, 67, 69–70, 80–87
definition of, 57–58
emotions and, 80–87
exercises on, 63–66, 74–75
limiting, 140–142, 149–153, 160, 179–180, 204–207
manifestation and, 21–22, 23, 35
on money, 149–153, 160
positive attitude and, 61–62, 65, 69, 72–74
self-esteem and, 59–60, 64, 68, 71–72
self-responsibility and, 58–59, 63, 68
on sexuality, 109–114
trust in universe and, 60–61, 64, 67, 68–69
victimhood and, 59
visualizations on, 70–74, 83–84
Body, physical
affirmations/visualizations on, 142–146
alignment of, 137–138
communication with, 125–130
core strength of, 137

Body, physical (*continued*)
  exercises on, 16, 126–130,
    131–134, 146
  flexibility of, 137
  healthy, 127
  limiting beliefs of, 140–142
  meditation and, 143
  mental attitude and, 139
  nutrition for, 138–139
  stamina of, 137
  treatment of, 16
  turnaround beliefs of,
    140–142
  vision for, 131–136

C

Change
  affirmations on, 69–70
  beliefs and, 62, 66, 67, 69–70,
    80–87
  in relationships, 95
Commitment, 85
  to affirmations/visualizations, 42
  in personal power, 42–43, 48
  sexuality and, 122
Communication
  with physical body, 125–130
  in relationships, 93, 96–98
  sexuality and, 120, 122
Consciousness, xiii, 126, 192–194,
    205, 206, 214
Discipline, 43, 49

E

Ego, 60, 205
Emotion(s)
  affirmations/visualizations on,
    83–84, 87, 90–91
  changing beliefs and, 80–87

  exercises on, 17–18, 85–87,
    90–91
  expressing, 17–18, 79–80
  letting go of, 88–91
  mental clearing of, 87–91
  sexuality and, 118
  visualizations on, 30, 83–84, 87,
    90–91
Environment, 44–45, 168

F

Fear
  exercises on, 102–107
  reinforcing, 24
  in relationships, 98–105
First Earth Run, 223, 225, 226, 227,
    228, 229
Forgiveness, xii, 6, 73

G

Gandhi, Mohandas, 187, 229
Gibran, Kahlil, 164

I

Inner guidance, 45–46, 50
Intuition, 176

K

Karma, 63, 206
Knowing, state of, 32–33

L

Love
  creating more, 15
  exercises on, 15
  personal power and, 46–47, 51
  in relationships, 96
  of self, 6, 8, 92–93, 165, 207

work with, 164, 166, 171, 173,
177–178
Lovemaking, 117–122

M

Manifestation
amount of time for, 34–35
beliefs and, 21–22, 23, 35
creative thought in, 20–21, 23
feedback on, 36
growing, 32–34
mental clearing in, 21–22, 23
of money, 154–158
not working, 35, 36–37
self-awareness and, 19, 28
using affirmations, 24–29
using visualization, 29–32
vision in, 22–23
worthiness and, 22
Meditation
affirmations/visualizations and,
214
inner guidance and, 45
on lightness, 55
physical body and, 143
spirituality and, 55, 186, 193,
200, 208
Miracles, 8

P

"Partners" (Gellman), 203–204
Passion, 6, 7, 16, 26
Positive attitude, 12, 61–62, 65,
72–74
Poverty consciousness, 148, 160
Power, personal
changing, 54–55
commitment in, 42–43, 48
definition of, 40

discipline in, 43, 49
exercises on, 48–52, 55–56
experiencing, 43
inner guidance and, 45–46, 50
lightness in, 46, 51
love and, 46–47, 51
personal truth and, 47, 52
sources of, 221–222
spirituality and, 4
support system and, 43–45, 50,
53
Power struggles, 94
Prosperity consciousness, 146

R

Relationship(s)
affirmations on, 96, 99–101, 105,
107
change in, 95
communication in, 93, 96–98
empowerment in, 5–6
exercises on, 15, 102–107
fears in, 98–105
fun in, 95
higher purpose in, 93
integrating male/female aspects
in, 94
love/pain in, 96, 100
personal space in, 94
power struggles in, 94
respect in, 95–96
self-esteem and, 60
spirituality in, 93
support systems for, 95
visualizations on, 102–107
vulnerability in, 96–98
with yourself, 92–93
Responsibility, 38. See also
Self-responsibility

S

Satyagraha, 187
Self-awareness. *See also* Awareness
  of beliefs, 39, 67, 74
  changing thoughts and, 217
  inner guidance and, 45
  manifestation and, 19, 28
Self-confidence, 174, 175
Self-esteem, 59–60, 64
  affirmations/visualizations on, 68,
    71–72
  beliefs and, 59–60, 64, 68, 71–72
  in relationships, 60
  vulnerability in, 99
Self-responsibility. *See also*
  Responsibility
  affirmations on, 68
  beliefs and, 58–59, 63, 68
  sexuality and, 109
Sensuality, 114–117
Seven Laws of Money (Phillips), 167
Sexuality
  affirmations/visualizations on,
    118, 122–124
  beliefs on, 109–114
  commitment and, 122
  communication and, 120, 122
  emotions and, 118
  exercises on, 114, 115–116,
    118–121, 123
  limiting, 110–111
  lovemaking and, 117–122
  monogamy and, 110
  self-responsibility and, 109
  sensuality and, 114–117
  spirituality and, 119
  stifling, 108
  turnaround beliefs of, 111–114
  visualizations and, 118

Spirituality
  acceptance in, 202
  affirmations/visualizations on,
    209
  aligning actions in, 201
  co-creating and, 202–204
  definition of, 186
  developing, 13
  ego and, 205
  exercises on, 189–190, 193–199
  gifts of, 194–199
  higher purpose and, 187–192,
    201, 207
  karma and, 206
  limiting beliefs of, 204–207
  meditation and, 55, 186, 193,
    200, 208
  money and, 149, 205
  nature and, 202
  in relationships, 93
  sexuality and, 119
  support system in, 201–202
  transcendence and, 192–193
  turnaround beliefs of, 204–207
  visualizations on, 189–191, 194–
    199, 209
Support systems, 43–45, 50, 53, 95,
  201–202, 217–219

T

Thought, creative, 20–21, 23
Transcendence, 192–193
Trust, 45, 60–61, 64, 67, 68–69
Truth, 47, 52

V

Victimhood, 7, 28, 59
Vision
  in manifestation, 22–23

Vision (*continued*)
 pathology and, 4
 for physical body, 131–136
 potential and, 3
 using, 11
Visualization(s)
 attention for, 212–213, 216–217
 collecting, 220
 commitment to, 42
 on core beliefs, 70–74
 definition of, 29
 on emotions, 30, 83–84, 87,
  90–91
 exercises on, 48–52
 feedback on, 36
 forms of, 213–214
 guided, 48–52
 interpreting, 52–-54
 manifestation using, 29–32
 meditation and, 214
 mental clearing in, 106
 on money, 159–163
 not working, 35, 36–37
 nourishing, 33
 number of, 215
 personal, 31
 on physical body, 142–146
 on positive attitude, 72–74
 on relationships, 102–107
 on self-esteem, 71–72
 on sexuality, 118, 122–124
 simple, 30–31
 on spirituality, 189–191, 194–
  199, 209
 updating, 215–216
 on work, 167–171, 179–184, 185
 writing, 31–32, 52
Vulnerability, 96–98, 99–100

W
Work
 affirmations/visualizations on,
  167–171, 179–184, 185
 choosing, 17
 dissatisfaction with, 165
 encouragement and, 174–175
 exercises on, 17, 167–171, 185
 fulfilled, 165
 intuition and, 176
 limiting beliefs of, 179–180
 with love, 164, 165, 166, 171,
  173, 177–178
 passionless, 165
 persistence and, 175–176
 personal appearance and, 176–
  177
 self-confidence and, 174, 175
 as stepping-stone, 165
 success plan for, 173–174
 transitioning between, 166
 turnaround beliefs of, 179–180
 valid, 81–82
 vision/plan for, 166–173
 visualizations on, 167–171
Worthiness, 5, 22, 38, 59, 64, 68, 83

About the Authors

David Gershon and Gail Straub created the Empowerment Workshop in 1981, and since then have offered it to thousands of people throughout the world. Their best-selling book, *Empowerment*, originally published in 1989 and translated into seven languages, has become a personal growth classic and is used worldwide as the basis for life coaching.

Building on their decades of teaching and research in 2001, David and Gail created the Empowerment Institute Certification Program to provide in-depth training in their state-of-the-art empowerment methodology for personal, organizational, community, and societal transformation. For information on the Empowerment Institute, please visit www.empowermentinstitute.net.

In 2010, Gail and David developed IMAGINE—a global initiative for the empowerment of women. In resource-poor settings around the world, women are empowered to envision and create new possibilities for themselves, their families, and their communities. Partner organizations in countries such as Afghanistan, Sudan (Darfur), Nigeria, India, and South Africa select women leaders to attend the Empowerment Institute, where they are trained to lead the Empowerment Workshop in their home countries. For more information, please visit www.imagineprogram.net.

David and Gail lecture widely, and their work and books have won many awards.

Other books by
David Gershon
Social Change 2.0
Low Carbon Diet
Green Living Handbook
The Livable Neighborhood
Journey for the Planet
Journey for the Planet Coaches'
  Guide

Water Stewardship
All Together Now
A Dream for Our World

Other books by Gail Straub
Returning to My Mother's House
The Rhythm of Compassion
Circle of Compassion